Empath
Healing

Simple Strategies on How to Help Nurture your Highly Sensitive Self for Emotional Healing and Personal Growth

Jean Tierney

© **Copyright 2019 by Jean Tierney - All rights reserved.**

The contents of this book may not be reproduced, duplicated or transmitted without direct written permission from the author.

Under no circumstances will any legal responsibility or blame be held against the publisher for any reparation, damages, or monetary loss due to the information herein, either directly or indirectly.

Legal Notice:

This book is copyright protected. This is only for personal use. You cannot amend, distribute, sell, use, quote or paraphrase any part or the content within this book without the consent of the author.

Disclaimer Notice:

Please note the information contained within this document is for educational and entertainment purposes only. Every attempt has been made to provide accurate, up to date and reliable complete information. No warranties of any kind are expressed or implied. Readers acknowledge that the author is not engaging in the rendering of legal, financial, medical or professional advice. The content of this book has been derived from various sources. Please consult a licensed professional before attempting any techniques outlined in this book.

By reading this document, the reader agrees that under no circumstances are is the author responsible for any losses, direct or indirect, which are incurred as a result of the use of information contained within this document, including, but not limited to, —errors, omissions, or inaccuracies.

Table of Contents

Introduction

Chapter 1: Understanding Your Empathic Nature

Chapter 2: Understanding and Developing Your Empathic Traits

Chapter 3: Applying Your Gifts Every Day

Chapter 4: Empaths and Relationships

Chapter 5: Coping Strategies for Empaths

Chapter 6: Protecting Yourself against Unwanted Emotions

Chapter 7: Empaths in the Workplace

Chapter 8: Dealing with Emotional Parasites (Narcissists and Energy Vampires) and Toxic People

Chapter 9: The Benefits of Recharging Through Solitude

Chapter 10: Raising Empathic Kids

Bonus Chapter: Dealing with the Media

Conclusion

Introduction

Being an empath or a highly sensitive person can present many challenges in your daily life. If you know or suspect that you are an empath, chances are that you have already noticed that you experience life in a much different way than others do. Perhaps, you find yourself struggling to engage in certain highly energetic or highly emotional environments, or maybe the people in your life have consistently told you that you are "too sensitive." These experiences, amongst others, are highly common for empaths who are living in a world where their gifts are not often honored or appreciated.

Empath Self-Discovery is going to support you with your journey of understanding your gift and learning how to develop it so that you can stop seeing your sensitivity as your weakness. The best way for you to use this book for your benefit is to read one chapter per day and apply the "quick start action step" as soon as you finish reading your chapter. Then, continue to practice that action step every single day, working it into your daily routine so that you can generate great success from it. Continue adding the quick start action steps into your daily routine until you have successfully added every single one. That way, you develop a strong foundation and create a snowballing effect within your empathic skillset so that you can start taking back control over your life and living a more empowered and joyous life.

As an empath, you are not required to live at the mercy of your sensitivity for the rest of your life, even if you live in a highly insensitive society that does not understand people with gifts like yours. You can choose to design your life in a more empowered manner and start living graciously, even if those around you never change. It is all accomplished through your mind and the way that you choose to perceive your life. Of course, that sounds easier in theory than it is in practice, but trust that with continuous practice, you can become an empowered empath who no longer struggles to survive in an insensitive society. Instead, you can begin thriving in any environment, and it all starts from creating a safe space where you can thrive from within.

If you are ready to rewrite your story and start living life as an empowered empath, this book is the perfect place for you to get started. Again, be sure to take your time and read through this book with the intention of reading one chapter and applying one new skill per day. This way, you do not overwhelm your inner empath and you are able to go ahead and master your gift, one day at a time. Please, enjoy!

Chapter 1: Understanding Your Empathic Nature

Chapter 1: Understanding Your Empathic Nature

You, empath, are a wildly beautiful gift that has been presented to the world before you, even if it does not yet feel that way. Although the collective does not see it, the gifts that you bring to this earth with you are beautiful treasures that help awaken us all to a glorious new way of life. It may feel overwhelming to know that you are a catalyst for change, but realize that this gift you share with the world is not one that falls entirely on your shoulders. In fact, there are many empaths just like you who are also here to help awaken the collective to it's most soft-hearted and sensitive nature that it has seemingly forgotten through recent generations.

Exploring exactly what your empathic gift is and how it works is imperative in helping you understand yourself and the gifts that you bring to the table. As an empath, one of the greatest gifts you can give yourself is the gift of connecting with others who are just like you so that you realize that your sensitivities are not strange or abnormal. In fact, they are perfectly normal based on the very nature of who you are. Let's take some time to explore exactly who you are as an empath and how this gift may be impacting your life so that you can see that you are not alone, even if it may feel like it at times.

What It Means to Be an Empath

Empaths have a paranormal ability that can support them in *feeling* the mental and emotional states of other individuals around them. As an empath, you may have a sense of what others are feeling before they even understand their own feelings, which can make it feel like you are reading their minds in a sense. Even though you may not have any cognitive awareness around where you are picking up on this information from, you may find yourself feeling it within your body in a way that may feel challenging to explain to others. In some cases, you may even feel the energy so intensely that you yourself start acting on the energy of the emotions before the person themselves actually picks up on it. For example, if you go into work one day and your boss is angry, you may begin experiencing intense anger yourself without having any logical reason or explanation as to where your anger has come from. Or, if you are watching the news and you see a story about a tragedy, you may find yourself feeling deeply saddened or even crying based on what you have watched. It is not abnormal for empaths to experience emotions to an intensely deep level, oftentimes, even exceeding the number of emotions being expressed by the person from whom they are absorbing the emotions from in the first place.

Being an empath is not the same as simply having or experiencing empathy. People who are merely experiencing empathy, on the other hand, only have a general sense of what the other person is feeling based on how they relate that experience to their own personal experiences. Individuals who are having true empathic experiences, however, are able to actually personally feel the immediate emotions of the other person, even if they cannot personally relate to the situation they are in. If you are an empath, you may find yourself feeling the intense pain of a tragedy that you have never personally experienced, to the point where it feels as though you yourself have been traumatized. This is why many empaths believe that their sensitivity is a burden rather than a gift because it can bring with it a great deal of pain if you are not yet educated on how to manage your gift.

Empathic gifts are not new phenomena by any means, as they have been identified and discussed for millennia through various texts, although it is frequently referred to with different names or theories. All in all, however, texts from the Bible to legends passed down through tribesmen have all discussed the phenomena in one way or another. If a religious and historical text is not enough to convince you that the phenomena you are experiencing are real, consider what scientific studies have shown regarding the empathic phenomena. Studies done in 2008 by Lacobani discovered an important part of the brain that is responsible for the empathic phenomena: the mirror neuron system. This system is the part of the brain responsible for helping people mirror other people's emotional experiences, and it was discovered that in empaths, the mirror neuron system is far more sensitive than in the average human. Through this, we can conclude that the gift of the empath has existed for a long time and that it is now backed by scientific evidence that proves that all of the historical text was onto something.

Why the Empathic Gift Exists

The truth is that no one person can tell you why you are an empath, or what exactly your gift is meant to serve. While many can speculate on what it may mean or why you may have been born as an empath, the reality is that only you can truly understand why you are an empath and what that means for you. You can learn more about your own unique empathic gifts by spending more time getting to know yourself and getting to understand what your unique purpose here on earth may be. Many believe that being an empath means that you are more highly gifted in your ability to help heal others in some way. These people may be on to something as if you look at other empaths in the society; you will recognize that even they seem to be on the path of healing others in one way or another.

Many empaths find themselves being called to:

- Be an energy healer or spiritual healer of sorts
- Fiercely defend and fight for a cause or charity; be a philanthropist
- Become a doctor, psychiatrist, or psychologist
- Enter the coaching industry to help others in some way
- Find a unique way to serve with their unique gifts

Empaths are regularly naturally called towards

purposes in life that, in one way or another; connect to the art of healing. Whether you are healing yourself, individuals, or larger bodies of society, your calling is likely to facilitate some degree of healing. The reason why empaths are perfect for this particular path is that they are able to feel where true healing is needed, which is a unique quality when it comes to healing. Empathic psychologists, for example, may have an intuitive ability to identify exactly where their patient is struggling and guide their healing in that direction, even if it is not obvious to the patient themselves.

The more you get to know yourself, the easier it is going to be for you to understand what your unique calling is alongside your empathic gifts. Fortunately, there is no one right answer which means that you can follow any path that your heart calls you towards. As you do, you will grow to know yourself in a more intimate and understanding manner, which will not only help you master your inner empath but will also help you master your emotional intelligence. Through these two forms of mastery, you can serve yourself in living a better life with the knowledge you require to protect yourself and maintain a sense of energetic and emotional well-being day in and day out.

How to tell that you are an Empath

If you have found yourself relating to some of the examples that have already been provided within this book, chances are you are an empath. However, let's take a deeper and clearer look into how you can tell that you are an empath and what this means in regards to who you are and what your unique needs are in life.

Your Intuition Is Incredibly Deep

If you are an empath, chances are that you experience an incredibly deep intuitive ability. Although you may not be able to explain it, you seem to just know things without ever having to be told or educated on them. It may even seem like you can predict the future, sometimes, based on the inner knowingness you have. For example, if someone is trying to surprise you with something, you may be able to tell in advance that a surprise is coming and, in some cases, you may even have a general idea of what that surprise will be. This is not necessarily because you are a psychic, but rather because you can "read" the energy that people are putting out through your extra senses, or your highly sensitive intuition, which are all a part of being an empath.

People Seem to Confide in You

Empaths often find themselves being turned to by just about everyone, whether they already know them or not. Friends, acquaintances, and even strangers may turn to you for help or confide in you about things that they admit they do not typically tell anyone about. You may even hear people often telling you things like "I don't know why I just said all of that" or "you are very easy to open up to!" The reason for that is because you are an empath and while others may not know what that means or even necessarily believe in it, they can sense it on some level. They can feel your gentle and empathic energy and know that by confiding in you, they will be opening up to someone who genuinely gets it, which helps them feel the compassion that they need to survive.

You Feel the Emotions of Others

If you are empathic, chances are that you can literally feel the emotions of others. Feeling the emotions of others likely stems from the mirror neuron system that we talked about in section 1.1 when you discovered exactly what it means to be an empath. When you feel the emotions of others, the intensity to which you feel it may vary depending on your own mood and the intensity to which the other person is feeling their emotions. Sometimes, you may simply feel a pang of anger or sadness when someone else is experiencing one of these emotions, and other times, you may feel intense anger or sadness in the presence of another emotional person. Your emotional experiences are not limited to anger or sadness, either, but can be felt in just about any emotion ranging from challenging or traumatic ones to uplifting and energetic ones. As such, you may find yourself being especially selective in surrounding yourself with people who have a positive and calm energy that is not overwhelming or burdensome on you personally. You may also find yourself struggling to spend time around your friends when they are having a hard time, not because you do not want to be supportive but because the influx of energy and emotions is overwhelming.

Public Places May Be Overwhelming

On the topic of overwhelm, you may be an empath if you find yourself avoiding public places because of the emotional overwhelm that you experience in these settings. You may experience genuine anxiety, or you may experience so many different types of emotions that it turns into anxiety because you do not know how to process all of the emotions and energies at once. It is not uncommon for empaths to live their lives as introverts as a way to separate themselves from the high energy and emotions of the busy world around them. Even empaths who wish to live the life of an extrovert may find themselves avoiding public places so that they can avoid the overwhelm, which can lead to even more challenging emotions to deal with, such as loneliness.

You Can Detect the Truth

Empaths have an uncanny ability to tell whether or not someone is telling the truth, and can often sniff out the truth like a dog can sniff out a piece of food. Your ability to detect the truth, even when it is not being clearly stated, stems from your deepened intuition and your ability to feel other people's emotions. When you are being lied to, you can likely feel that you are being lied to and you may even be able to detect what the truth actually is, even if the other person has not shared it with you yet.

You May Feel Unexplained Physical Symptoms

Beyond emotional absorption, empaths also have a tendency to experience the physical symptoms of others as well. It is not uncommon for empaths to report feeling the physical symptoms of those around them such as headaches, pains, fatigue, or other physical symptoms without any logical explanation as to why. For example, if someone was to break their ankle and have ankle pains, you may experience sudden intense pain in your ankle without any logical reason why.

The News May Upset You

Empaths often find themselves feeling incapable of watching the news or paying attention to popular media because the media often features traumatic information that can be heavy for the empath to endure. If you are an empath, you may find yourself avoiding popular media because of the amount of emotional struggle you face after watching, listening to, or reading it. Some empaths also find that they avoid television shows, movies, and books that feature any form of tragedy or violence because of the energy and emotions that they experience following that exposure.

You Prefer Holistic and Natural to Anything Else

Empaths are not only highly sensitive in a mental and emotional sense but also in a physical sense. It is not uncommon for empaths to favor natural alternatives because the energy in those natural options feels significantly more calming and supportive than the energies in anything else. This preference for natural and holistic alternatives often manifests in everything from how empaths choose to approach their health and wellness to how empaths choose to purchase their textiles and home goods.

You Are Creative

Empaths are known for being particularly gifted

in their creative expression, and it often manifests in many different ways. If you are particularly drawn into the creative arts in one way or another, chances are this is a manifestation of your empathic gifts. This creative expression may show up in your life in many ways, from a natural talent when it comes to drawing or painting to an incredible ability to invent new technology or tools. Empaths are often highly gifted with creativity in many different ways, so you may see this creative expression showing up differently throughout your life.

You Crave Solitude

Empaths, even ones who identify as extroverts, often find themselves craving solitude, because in solitude, there is no need to worry about being exposed to intense emotions or energies. If you find yourself often retreating into your alone time as an opportunity to rest and recharge from your daily experiences, you are likely experiencing the common craving for solitude that empaths experience. This craving for solitude is not just a desire but an actual need because it allows you the opportunity to release the energy and emotion that you have absorbed from your daily experiences. During this time, you can increase your ability to rest and recharge by practicing grounding meditations and intentionally unplugging from the world around you.

You May Have an Addictive Personality

Empaths have a tendency to lean towards addictive personalities. Typically, an empath will lean towards using drugs or alcohol as away to "numb" the mind to avoid experiencing the uncomfortable symptoms of being an empath. Typically, substance abuse will only help temporarily and then it will begin to produce greater problems for the empath in the long run, which can make them a dangerous bandaid for a problem. Alcohol and drugs are not the only addictions that empaths will have, either. You might find yourself using other obsessions or compulsions as your crutch as well, such as using your phone or rubbing a certain spot on your body.

You Likely Crave Learning and Are Curious

Empaths tend to be interested in learning more and understanding the world around them, which can lead to an inquisitive nature. Because the sensation of learning more and understanding more feels really good, empaths tend to really crave living in this space of understanding. If you find that you are drawn to courses, school, reading, and other learning tools, this is likely a symptom of you being an empath.

You Love Nature and Animals

Empaths connect with nature and animals in a way that most people do not, which is why empaths tend to have a deep love and appreciation for nature and animals. You may feel as though you are receiving messages from nature or from animals, even though you cannot explain how or why these messages are being shown to you. The reality is: you are an empath and your intuitive knowingness is responsible for this experience. Just like you can sense or feel other people's emotions and energies, you can also sense or feel the energies of something like a tree, or a horse. For this reason, it may be fun for you to connect with nature and animals and enjoy their presence.

You Root for The Underdog

Empaths tend to root for the underdog because they can feel the energy of that particular person and they want everyone to feel good. When they know that someone is being wronged or is not receiving their due justice, an empath will always do their best to root for them and support them in receiving their justice. You might look back on your life and realize that you have always been the one rooting for the person who was just starting out, or who was being bullied or wronged by the people around them. Although others could not seem to see or sense it, you knew inside that they were genuinely a good person and that they deserved the opportunity to feel good, too. This is because you are an empath.

You Like Loose, Flowing Clothes

Because empaths are so sensitive, having clothes that are tight fitting or uncomfortable based on their texture is almost always a no-go for empaths. The idea of dressing for beauty rather than comfort makes no sense to you as you literally feel like you are being suffocated by the clothes that you are wearing if they are not comfortable. You may like the idea of modern fashion, but any time you actually try to wear it you may feel uncomfortable to the point of being unable to accept it. This is because, as an empath, your senses are far more sensitive so simple things like this can be overwhelming and uncomfortable.

You Cannot Tolerate Clutter

Much like you cannot tolerate tight fitting or uncomfortable clothes, you may also find that being around clutter makes you uncomfortable to the point of not being able to engage in a normal functioning life. If your house is messy, or if you go to someone else's house who is, you may start to feel an increase in your anxiety and overwhelm. Some people may call you picky or uptight, but to you it is an energetic thing that you may not always be able to explain to those who just don't get it.

Further Discovery

There are many more signs that you may be an empath, all of which can be discovered by taking a simple empathic test that measures whether or not you are a true empath. A great test that you can take to discover whether or not you are an empath is the "Empath Test" which can be found by going to the website www.empathtest.com. There, you can take a short 5-minute test that will help you discover whether or not you are an empath.

Your Quick Start Action Step: Test Yourself

Now that you have a general understanding of what an empath is, what it is like to be one and how you can discover if you are one, it's time for you to take action! Before you proceed, you will want to make absolutely certain that you are an empath so that the tools you start applying truly do support you and your needs. So, your quick action step today is to schedule aside fifteen minutes of your time to complete the Empath Test and discover whether or not you are an empath!

If you are an over-achiever and would like to do more today, I encourage you to start looking for areas where your empathic symptoms show up in your life. By getting a general idea of how and where these symptoms are showing up for you, you can start to become aware of the fact that some of your perceived weaknesses may instead simply be your empathic gift. Drawing awareness to these areas of your life allows you to start getting a clearer understanding around your empathic gift so that you can start accepting yourself in a more complete way.

Chapter 2: Understanding and Developing Your Empathic Traits

Chapter 2: Understanding and Developing Your Empathic Traits

You now know that you are likely an empath, but you may still be wondering what that means exactly. How have your empathic traits been impacting your life already, what are they meant to accomplish, and how can you actually use them to your advantage? These may be questions that you are asking yourself as you seek to discover how you can master being an empath. In this chapter, we are going to explore exactly what traits you may have as an empath, what they are meant to accomplish, and how you can start mastering them so that they no longer wreak havoc in your life. Think of it like Harry Potter learning to embody his magical talents: when they are not under control, chaos ensues, but when he begins to discover how he can control them, suddenly, his entire world changes. Although your gifts and Harry Potter's gifts are not the same, the importance of you mastering your gifts to avoid overwhelm and chaos is just as important.

How to Engage in Your Empathic Self-Discovery

Engaging in self-discovery can be both exciting and overwhelming as you dig deeper into the understanding of what it means to be an empath for you personally. As you engage in your empathic self-discovery, I encourage you to take your time and use a journal along the way so that you can track your experiences. It is not uncommon to experience moments throughout the journey of your self-discovery where, suddenly, parts of your identity or your reality begin to make sense to you. This can be both liberating and overwhelming as you begin to come to terms with parts of yourself or your reality that you may have neglected, ignored, or even been ashamed of in the past. Taking your time and giving yourself permission to move at your own pace is imperative as it will ensure that you do not rush yourself and experience energetic or emotional overwhelm as a result.

I also encourage you to see your self-discovery

as a journey and not a destination, as you will always be on the path of self-discovery in your lifetime. Instead of hoping for some form of finite outcome or end result from your journey, pay attention to each step of the process and see what that process has to offer you. The more you pay attention and listen to your inner self and intuition, the easier it will be for you to prevent overwhelm and genuinely enjoy the process while also gaining as much as you possibly can from it. As an empath, moving at this slower pace is especially important as your self-discovery journey often will include healing and deeper emotional understanding that can take time for you to work through. Do not pressure yourself into moving any faster than you feel is reasonable so that you do not inadvertently worsen the symptoms of your empathic gifts, rather than understand and master them.

How Your Understanding Improves Your Self-Awareness

As an empath, having a sense of self-awareness around yourself and your gifts is imperative if you want to experience personal growth and joy in your life. Often, empaths do not understand themselves or their own needs so they strive to fit into a society that does not accommodate their unique sensitivities and needs. As a result, they end up feeling extremely out of place and chronically uncomfortable in a life that does not fit them.

When you develop your self-awareness, you increase your ability to accept yourself and have greater confidence and understanding of your gifts. This means that any time you experience empathic overwhelm, you will know exactly what you need to do in order to combat it and move forward in your life. As an empath, having a high level of self-awareness matches having a high level of sensitivity, which results in you being more likely to experience a better life overall.

How You Can Develop Your Empathic Traits

Developing your empathic traits starts by understanding which ones you have the most and choosing to take control over them in a more powerful and meaningful way. If you want to recall which empathic traits you have, go back to the quiz you did after chapter one, then highlight which traits you seem to have the most of. This way, you can focus on your unique talents and really develop your ability to work your empathic gift for the greater good.

Once you know which talents you are going to be developing, you can go ahead and start following the strategies below so that you can begin developing your empathic gifts.

Development Step 1: Educate Yourself

The first step that you want to take towards developing your abilities is to educate yourself. Empaths have many different abilities which are often identified as being one of the "Clairsenses" or "clear senses" which are a set of eight paranormal senses that empaths have. These clear senses refer to the paranormal extension of your existing five senses, as well as three additional senses that are used to help you sense energy around you through your intuition and instinct.

Each empath has at least one of the clairsenses awakened to some degree, as you likely picked up on through your empath testing. The most common one to be possessed by empaths is claricognizance, or clear knowingness, which relates to your clear ability to tell how someone else is feeling even if they do not tell you about it.

Educating yourself further on what it means to be an empath, where your gifts come from, and how they feel to have them is important. This type of self-education is going to allow you to have a greater understanding of what each of your gifts are and how they can be used to help you do better in life. This book is a great place to start, but I encourage you to continue educating yourself on what it means to be an empath until you reach the point of feeling a deep sense of understanding around yourself and your gifts.

When it comes to developing your gifts, this deeper sense of self-awareness will be incredibly important and will help you succeed in being able to intentionally control your gifts.

There are many ways that you can further your education around what it means to be an empath and where your gifts come from. Podcasts, blogs, and many influential people in the spiritual industry talk about empathic gifts and how you can harness yours and use them for your highest good. The more you surround yourself with these resources, the more you will understand yourself and the more connected you will feel to other empaths who have similar experiences to yours.

Development Step 2: Practice Shielding Yourself

Aside from further educating yourself on your empathic gifts, you should also be learning how to shield yourself. Personal energetic shields are a tool that empaths use to help protect their energy fields from the energy of those around them. This tool is imperative in helping you enjoy public places or highly energetic environments without feeling so overwhelmed by the people around you. There are a few ways that you can build an energetic shield for yourself, though only one seems to be the most commonly used by empaths on a day-to-day basis. The difference between shields is typically based on the intensity of the shield more so than the shape of it or how it is designed, so you can take the following guidance and adjust it if you need a stronger shield at any time.

To get started in energetic shielding, you simply need to begin by meditating and grounding yourself. Then, once you are completely relaxed, envision a white ball of energy anchoring into the center of your body, into your solar plexus. From there, imagine that the ball of white energy starts growing outwards, slowly encompassing your entire body with white energy, and sweeping anything unwanted out of your energy field. Once the ball grows to the point where it extends a few feet above your head and below your feet, and evenly out all around you, you can relax and envision that energy anchoring itself in so that it stays with you. Mentally declare that you are keeping your shield up and that energy that does not belong to you is not allowed to penetrate and attempt to hijack your personal energy field. Then, once you are confident in your shield, you can end your meditation and go about your day.

As you go about your daily experiences, check in on your energy shield every now and again and make sure that it is still working for you. If it is not, take some time to recreate your shield so that it can start protecting you once again. Early on, you may find yourself needing to recreate your energy shield on a regular basis to protect you from the energy around you, especially because you are not yet strong with wielding your shield. However, as you get stronger and you become more accustomed to creating and maintaining your shield, it will become easier for you to maintain it for good. Over time, you should only need to reinforce it, not actually rebuild it, as you should become strong enough for it to continue working for you in a more powerful manner.

If you need your shield to be stronger, simply lay more intention into the shield as you develop it. Take your time in building your shield and request that no energy may come through, or that only the energy you ask for may come through. If you are in a negative place, such as around a toxic energy vampire or narcissist, consider making a shield that will allow no known or unknown energy through to avoid having unexpected energetic attacks. You will learn more about special shields and management strategies for energy vampires later on, but this will give you a general idea in how you can use your shield for your best success.

Development Step 3: Reprogramming Your Beliefs

At this stage, you have developed a deeper self-awareness and a sense of how you can protect yourself from others, so now it is time for you to start reprogramming your beliefs. Your beliefs have a major impact on what you feel and how you live your life, so spending time reprogramming your beliefs is important if you want to protect yourself against any of the harms that may come with being an empath. Furthermore, reprogramming your beliefs can also empower you which mean that you will have a better chance at experiencing more positivity and optimism around your gifts rather than negativity and burdens.

Reprogramming your beliefs are going to come in two steps as an empath: first, you need to reprogram general beliefs that have been taught to you by others. For example, the beliefs that you are too sensitive, weak, incapable, incompetent, different, or strange should all be considered. If anyone has bullied you and you have been penalized for other aspects of who you are because of being an empath, honestly address those beliefs and include them in your reprogramming. You are also going to need to reprogram any pre-existing beliefs that you may have around being an empath. For example, if you believe that empaths are weak, that they have to absorb other peoples' energies, or that they are incapable of going out in public and enjoying themselves, you will want to reprogram these as well. Re-programming your belief system ultimately allows you to develop your own inner manifesto around what it means to be an empath and how you are choosing to allow this gift to empower and uplift you rather than burden you.

You should write down all of the beliefs you have around who you are, your sensitive nature, and what it means to be an empath so that you are clear on everything that is holding you back. Then, you should go ahead and start the reprogramming process. The reprogramming process happens in two phases: uprooting your current beliefs and replacing them with new beliefs. In order to uproot your current beliefs, you will need to begin by identifying why they are likely to be untrue and finding evidence to convince yourself that they are meaningless. For example, if you believe that you are too sensitive, consider using all of your strengths and successes in life to prove that you are not too sensitive. By finding evidence that combats what you are being told, you can start teaching your mind to stop believing in your current beliefs because they no longer hold up as true.

Then, you can go on to start using affirmations and positive mantras to help you reprogram your mind with new positive beliefs. You can easily do this by creating a mantra that reinforces your new desired beliefs and allows you to feel confident in them. You can also start finding evidence that proves your new desired beliefs so that you are able to convince yourself that they are, in fact, true. For example, if you want your new belief to be that you are courageous and strong, you could create a mantra such as "I am courageous and strong" and affirm it to yourself on a regular basis. When you do, start recounting all of the times that you exerted your courage and strength to help you overcome a challenge in your life to convince yourself that it is true.

It will likely take some time for you to start reprogramming your inner belief system and have it actually stick, so do not worry if you do not see results right away or feel better immediately. Our beliefs are created from a repetitive statement or piece of information that was told to us consistently over time, either directly or through someone else's behaviors and actions. So, reprogramming your current beliefs requires you to go ahead and start reinforcing your new beliefs through repetition so that they can effectively take over for your old beliefs.

Development Step 4: Grounding Yourself Completely

The next step that you need to learn in developing your empathic gifts is how to ground completely. Grounding yourself is going to give you the ability to ensure that you are able to completely eliminate unwanted energies from your energy field at any given time. You will need to incorporate two styles of grounding into your life: a more standard daily grounding practice and a grounding practice that you will use on-the-go. When you are able to ground in both ways, you can ensure that any time unwanted energy breaches your energy field, you can eliminate it from your field immediately.

Your more intentional grounding practice should be done every single night before bed to ensure that you are not holding onto unwanted energies as you go into your restful sleep. You can also do it in the morning to completely ground from any energy that you may have picked up on in your sleep if you wish. This way, you can start and end your day with clean and cleared energies that are not going to be overwhelming or too stressful for you to face.

You can engage in an intentional grounding practice by relaxing into a meditative state and then requesting that any energy within your body leave immediately. You can do this by sitting or lying down somewhere relaxing and closing your eyes so that you can engage in some simple breathwork, breathing into the count of 8 and out to the count of 8. As you do, imagine your body completely relaxing and all of the energies in and around your energy field coming into your conscious awareness. Then, once you are completely relaxed, envision a root extending from your tailbone into the center of the earth that takes away all unwanted energies that are in your energy field. This root should completely draw out everything, leaving you with nothing except for your own personal energies and the energies that are required to help you live your best life each day.

If you feel extremely bogged down throughout your day, such as if you are having a particularly challenging day and you need to ground again, you can also use this more traditional and intense grounding method. This will help you eliminate each unwanted energy that you may have in your field that could be wreaking havoc on you. If, however, you find that you are just in need of a simple and quick grounding technique to help you in an on-the-go situation, you can try using the following method.

Get comfortable wherever you are, whether you are standing or sitting, and plant your feet firmly on the floor. Then, visualize a connection taking place between your feet and the earth, forming a root-like connection that you can release any unwanted energies through. Once the connection is made, you can simply request any unwanted energies from your energy field be removed and not welcomed back into your energy space. If you are in an active situation where unwanted energy is being thrown your way consistently, such as if you are around a narcissist, visualize this rooted connection staying in place and removing unwanted energy out of your field at all times. This way, you are consistently moving out any unwanted energy and it is not getting trapped in your energy field and weighing you down.

Development Step 5: Reading Other People

Once you have learned how to protect and ground yourself, and you start developing a positive confidence in your gifts, it is time for you to start learning how to read other people through them! The process of reading people is heavily based on your ability to listen to your intuition and really tune in to what energies they are giving off and trusting what you are receiving intuitively through that energy. It can take some time to develop trust and confidence in your intuition, but once you have, it can be one of the most powerful tools for you to call on throughout your life.

The best way to start playing with your intuition is to start playing games with it and building your ability to both listen to it and trust it when you begin recognizing what it feels like inside of you. As an empath, chances are that you have been pushed to ignore this voice for so long that you may not remember what it sounds like or you may instinctively ignore it for fear of what might happen if you do listen to it. So, one of your biggest challenges will be tuning back in and trusting in what it sounds like so that you can gain information from it and use it to your advantage.

A great way to start reading other people and developing your intuition at the same time is to start by anticipating what someone else's energy is and then looking for clues that your intuition was right. For example, say you feel an angry energy to someone even though they have not yet shown any signs of anger, you can then start looking for signs of anger in this person to validate whether or not you were correct. You can also start reading people by seeing if you can predict what someone is going to say, or what nature their conversation is going to be about, based on what their energy is. For example, if someone tells you that they want to tell you about something serious practice reading the energy to see if they are going to tell you something serious that is exciting, or something serious that is upsetting. Then, validate that based on what they actually tell you and see whether you were right or not.

You can also practice honing in on your intuition by playing games on your own, which can help you develop your ability to read energy which then helps you read the energy of actual people. A great way to do this is to take a deck of cards and lay one face down on the table and then see if you can feel the energy of what number, suit, or color that card is before you flip it over. The more you practice, the more you are going to get a sense for what energies feel like, how you read them, and what your intuition tells you to do.

When it comes to these types of reading games, it is important to understand that your intuition is not always going to lead you to the right answer. You might predict someone's energy or conversational topic incorrectly, or you might find yourself consistently guessing the cards wrong. Understand that your goal here is not so much to get it right as to start listening to your intuition so that you can get a clear sense of what it sounds like and what it feels like when you follow your intuition. Later on, this will support you in intuitively navigating and avoiding unwanted situations in a more wholesome way that does not drain you.

Your Quick Start Action Step: A Day in The Life

Now, it is time for your quick action step! In order for you to really start understanding and developing your gifts, you are going to need time to practice them! Today, I encourage you to set aside three ten-minute windows of time for you to start practicing developing your empathic gifts so that you can use them at your own will. In the first window, you are going to practice building your shield that you can carry with you throughout the day, thus helping you begin to learn how to keep out unwanted energies. In the second window, you are going to play the intuition game with a deck of cards so that you can start learning how to trust and work in alignment with your intuition. In the third window, you are going to completely ground your energies from your day.

This is not only a short and simple series of practices that should require no more than 30 minutes of your time, but it is also a great routine to get into. As you start focusing on keeping yourself grounded and protected and learning how to develop your intuition, your life as an empath will improve tenfold. It will become much easier for you to enjoy a higher quality of life and stop struggling in the face of challenges so that you can begin thriving as an empowered empath.

Chapter 3: Applying Your Gifts Every Day

Chapter 3: Applying Your Gifts Every Day

As you continue practicing how to develop your empathic gifts, you are going to want to start learning about how you can apply them in your everyday life. This chapter is going to show you how you can begin taking your development to the next level and experiencing significantly more joy and empowerment from your empathic gifts. This level of integration is going to help you begin to overcome some of those more challenging symptoms you have been experiencing in your life so that you can start enjoying yourself once more.

Finding Where Your Day Can Be Improved

The first thing you are going to need to do in order to integrate your empathic gifts into your daily life is to start looking out for areas where your day can be improved. As an empath, you may be so used to living your days stressed out and overwhelmed that you may not even be clear as to where or when those feelings start to leak into your daily experiences. Getting clear on where these energies are coming from, when, why, and how it feels when they begin is going to help you get clear on what it is that you want to improve with your daily integration.

Keeping an empathic journal is a great way for you to start identifying areas of your life where you are being impacted by your gifts so that you know where you want to place your focus when it comes to intentionally incorporating them. You can keep just a small journal with you or even a note in your phone, where you will record the time of day when the energy came up, what was happening, what you were thinking, and how you were feeling. After a while, you will start to see trends in your energy, where your energy is absorbing unwanted energies, and how you might be leaving yourself vulnerable to these particular forms of energy.

Giving Yourself Permission to Start One Step at a Time

The next step in incorporating your empathic gifts into your daily life is giving yourself permission to do it at your own pace. One of the biggest mistakes empaths make is trying to change their entire lives in one go which, while admirable, can be extremely exhausting and overwhelming. The truth is, as you go about using your gift to empower you rather than allowing others to use it to exploit you, there is going to be some difficulties for you to endure. You are going to have to start learning how to navigate the energies of people as they grow frustrated with their newfound inability to exploit you, which takes some time to get used to. At first, you might find yourself giving in despite having all of the best practices in place and this can bring about frustration and anger within you, as well as the need to ground from the unwanted energies of the other person. Giving yourself permission to go slowly and make mistakes along the way ensures that you do not set your expectations too high and bite off more than you can reasonably chew.

The best way to give yourself permission and

really mean it is to first declare that you are giving yourself permission to take things slowly and at your own pace. Then, create a mantra that you will use any time that you are actively put in a position where you need to give yourself permission to slow down and navigate it at your own pace. For example, if you are in a situation where you habitually find yourself letting others take advantage of you, give yourself permission to navigate it at your own pace and do your best to change the situation as much as possible. If you find yourself struggling to make changes, take the pressure off by letting yourself know that there is no need to get it perfect the first time. The more you practice putting up shields and setting boundaries, the easier it will be for you to do so with greater assertiveness and intention in the future. There is nothing wrong with going slow and at your own pace, and do not be afraid to repeat your personal mantra to yourself anytime you start feeling like this is not true. Be gentle with yourself.

Steps to Integrating Your Empathic

Gifts Daily

You are now ready to see what it looks like to start integrating your empathic gifts into your daily life! What this will look like from day to day will vary, depending on what situations you are entering and what is expected of you during these situations. For that reason, rather than giving you a routine or schedule for how you can incorporate your empathic gifts into every single day, I am going to give you some tips you can use to start incorporating it in unique experiences. Then, you can start relying on these anytime you need them to help you navigate new situations and experience greater comfort and empowerment in your life!

Step 1: Read the Energy of the Day

The first thing you can do each morning, aside from creating your shield and grounding yourself, is read the energy of that day. Many empaths report being able to feel the energy of any given day based on the energy that the general collective is giving off. Spending some time reading that energy each morning can help you get a sense of what you might stand to face as you go about your daily experiences.

You can read the energy of any given day during your morning meditation by simply asking your intuition what energies are present that day and how they may impact you. Then, trust any information that comes through intuitively, even if it does not necessarily make sense to you at that time. You may not have any words you can use to verbally describe what the energy is like, but instead, you may have a general feeling inside that gives you an idea of what to expect. This is plenty enough to give you an idea of what energies to look out for and how you may be able to prepare yourself against them, simply by being able to expect that they will arise.

Step 2: Read the Energy of People

The next thing that you can consider doing on a daily basis is reading the energy of the people you encounter. Slowing down at the beginning of every interaction and taking a few moments to read the energy of the people around you will give you an opportunity to get an idea of how they may be feeling that day. This is going to help you not only get a sense for how your interactions may be, but also for where energy may be coming if you start to experience unexpected energies in your own body. For example, if you know that your spouse was particularly happy that morning and you have an unexplained feeling of elation all day long, it may be the energy that you picked up on from your spouse.

You can also use this as an opportunity to read the energy of new people that you encounter to help you determine whether or not they are a good person to engage and interact with. If you are looking to make new friends or network with new people, for example, you can use your intuition to help you determine whether or not it will be a positive experience. This is a great way to start picking up on the energy of energy parasites such as narcissists early on so that you can avoid building relationships with them right from the start.

Step 3: Create a Safe Grounding Space for Yourself

You likely already crave solitude to some degree, so why not feed into that desire and create a safe grounding space for yourself? You can do this by either creating a grounding sanctuary within your home or by finding a place outside of your home that you like to retreat to. Or, if you want to get really fancy, you can do both!

If you want to create a grounding sanctuary in your home, consider choosing one room or an area in one room where you can fill it with things that are relaxing and grounding. Use crystals, live plants, calming incenses, soft fabrics, uplifting pictures, and other great and relaxing tools to help you make the area more inviting. Then, begin practicing your daily grounding experiences in that specific area in your home every single time. What will end up happening is that you find yourself connecting more deeply with that particular area, so just entering it will be grounding, thus making intentional grounding meditations in that sanctuary even more powerful.

If you would like to incorporate a destination into your grounding experiences, consider choosing one that is nearby and that you can attend frequently. A local park or a bird sanctuary may be a great opportunity for you to find a local place that you can retreat to and experience grounding energies in. This type of grounding destination can be particularly helpful if you are someone who finds that their own home tends to become overwhelmed with exhausting or troublesome energies.

Step 4: Make Experiences Richer

One great way that you can incorporate your gift into your daily life is through making your experiences richer using your extra senses. Think of it this way: if you can experience someone else's energies and emotions that deeply, imagine what else you can experience that deeply? See how intensely you can experience meals, laughter, nostalgia, and tranquility. Look for opportunities to uplift yourself through these experiences and see if you can find ones that routinely makes you feel better, particularly if you are having a difficult day. In doing so, not only does this become a fun opportunity for you to experience life more joyously, but it also allows you to begin finding experiences that can reliably lift you out of a troublesome mood.

Your Quick Start Action Step: Experience Intensely

Your quick action step today is to find one experience that you can fully immerse yourself into and let yourself be swept away from it just like you are by other people's energies or emotions when you are not grounded and protected. Find one activity that you can fully immerse yourself into, and see just how much energy you can draw out of that experience and what that energy feels like. If it begins to feel too intense or overwhelming, take a few minutes to ground yourself before either going back into the activity or switching to something more calming.

The more you practice getting the most out of life by experiencing energies in this positive way, the better your life is going to feel overall. It is well worth your time to start learning how to become deeply mindful of and engaged in each moment in your life so that you can stop retreating and dissociating from your experiences. This is going to help you reconnect with your daily life and start living for you again, and not for everyone around you.

Chapter 4: Empaths and Relationships

Chapter 4: Empaths and Relationships

As an empath, navigating relationships in your life can be challenging, especially if you are not actively in tune with your intuition. Empaths have a tendency to find themselves being sucked into unhealthy relationships as a result of their desire to "save" the people around them. This is not so much as an inner desire to be a savior as a symptom of feeling other people's energies as deeply as they do and experiencing deep and intense compassion for them. Even so, empaths can be particularly vulnerable to abusive relationships as a result of this deep inner compassion.

Learning how to navigate your relationships effectively is important if you are going to be engaging in relationships that allow you to thrive as an empath. You need to learn how to identify toxic relationships, how to handle yourself when toxic behaviors arise, and what you can do to ensure that your needs are also being met in your relationships.

Navigating Relationships as an Empath

As an empath, you need to be particularly cautious about the relationship that you enter in your life. Even seemingly harmless relationships such as those that you share with your coworkers or your boss can quickly become toxic if you are not careful. If you have already noticed this toxicity arising in these relationships, you may find yourself struggling to decide how to proceed so that you can avoid being taken advantage of or emotionally or energetically abused. In that case, you need to learn how to navigate your relationships with others.

The first and primary tool that you need to rely on in every single relationship is your intuition. As you know, your intuition is your superpower as an empath, and learning how to behave in alignment with your intuition is imperative if you are going to avoid unwanted experiences. If you find yourself in a relationship that you are questioning, in terms of toxicity, chapter 8 will be extremely helpful for you in navigating these relationships. Otherwise, your intuition will allow you to discover when people are being genuine towards you or when they are breaching your boundaries. Many times, empaths will enter relationships with perfectly healthy people and will accidentally teach those people to ignore their boundaries because they are inexperienced with having and upholding boundaries. As an empath, you are going to need to start intuitively deciding where your boundaries are and feeling into it any time you believe that your boundaries have been breached. That way, you can ensure that you are asserting yourself when you need to and that you are avoiding turning otherwise healthy relationships into toxic ones through your own toxic behaviors.

Troubles That May Arise in Relationships

As an empath, one of the most common troubles that will arise is your tendency to attract narcissists and other energetic vampires into your life. They seem to be able to sense the empathic energies of people and will quickly take advantage of an empath they meet as soon as they meet one, including yourself. If you want to avoid being taken advantage of, you have to be willing to lean into your intuition and genuinely pay attention to the signs of how people are treating you and what it truly means.

The second trouble that commonly arises for empaths is the tendency to become codependent because of how challenging it can be to navigate social situations on their own. You may find yourself clinging to one or two people who you are particularly close to who make you feel comfortable when you are together. In some cases, this may be a healthy friendship or relationship, but in other cases, it may turn into you becoming dependent on this other individual to help you in public experiences. Even if they are a genuine and kind-hearted person, this type of dependency can lead to many troubles for you, so it is ideal to avoid these types of codependent relationships with people.

Your Needs as an Empath

As an empath, you have unique needs in relationships that may be quite different from the needs of those around you. Because you are more sensitive and vulnerable to the energies of those around you, you need to be ready to identify what your needs are and assert them as you move through your relationship. Remember, your needs are going to be quite different from others and the people you enter relationships with may not be empaths themselves, meaning that you are going to have to be ready to stand up for yourself. You will need to ensure that you are in a relationship where you feel confident in standing up for yourself, and where you standing up for yourself are honored by those around you.

Below are the five needs that you must consider before entering a relationship with anyone, or continuing a relationship with anyone if you are an empath.

You Need to Maintain Your Alone Time

As an empath, you are going to need to ensure that you do not fall into the vices of codependency by maintaining your alone time and learning to stay emotionally and energetically sound on your own. It can be easy to find a person that you feel safe around and who "gets" you and want to exclusively spend your time with this person, but falling into this habit can be dangerous. If you are not careful, you may find yourself building up codependency towards others, which can extremely inhibit your own ability to feel complete and whole by yourself.

In addition to you personally choosing to maintain your alone time, you also need to ensure that the other half in your relationships are willing to allow you to enjoy your alone time as well. For some people, the amount of alone time that you need or when it is needed may seem unreasonable or confusing to them. It is important that they understand that even if it does not make sense to them, they still need to respect your need for solitude. They should know that during this time, you will not be available to talk, spend time together, or be around anyone aside from yourself because you need this time to recharge.

If you are in a relationship where this is not yet being honored, make sure that you are honest with this person about your need for alone time and that you make it clear as to why you need it. If they do not understand terms like "empath," simply say that you feel overwhelmed when you are around too much at once and you occasionally need complete solitude to recharge. Sometimes, saying it in a very plain and straightforward way can help it make more sense to other people.

You Need to Be Heard and Respected

In any relationship you enter, you need to be heard and respected in that relationship. This is true for any relationship, but as an empath, you may find it challenging to assert yourself in this way and you might find yourself willingly letting other people ignore you or disrespect your wishes. This is not necessarily due to a lack of self-respect or a lack of desire to be cared for, but because you struggle to assert yourself for fear of what emotional and energetic backlash you might face. It may feel uncomfortable for you to speak up and declare that you do not feel heard or respected, which might mean that instead of asserting yourself, you say nothing and try to "make do" with what happens.

If you are entering a new relationship, pay close attention to how that person listens and how they respect you after you have voiced your needs or concerns. If they listen and they respect you, chances are that they are a positive person to enter a relationship with. If they do not, however, or they respect you for a short period of time and then later disrespect you or say it was "too big of a request" (this is common with narcissists), then you should avoid this relationship. These types of relationships can become emotionally and mentally draining and are especially dangerous to vulnerable empaths.

If you are in a relationship where you feel as though you are not being heard or respected by the other person, you need to speak up for yourself and voice your concerns. Let them know that you are trying to be heard but that you feel as though they are not listening to you, or that they hear you but they are not respecting your wishes. If they change, your problem may have been inside of a communication error that you were struggling with. If they don't, you may be in a relationship with a narcissist or an energy parasite and you need to end that relationship or minimize your exposure to that person as much as possible.

You Need to Stay Open and Honest

Aside from having the other person listen to you more intently and clearly, you also need to be willing to speak up for yourself and do your best to be heard. As an empath, you may feel that you have been taught to stay quiet or say nothing for fear of what energetic or emotional consequences you might face if you told the truth. This is highly common, but it can also be highly destructive to you if you are trying to engage in more positive relationships but keep finding yourself being steamrolled by those in your life.

As you begin to develop new relationships in your life, seek to start off on the foot of being honest and upfront with the person you are entering a relationship with. Rather than getting into the habit of minimizing yourself or shrinking yourself for their benefit, get into the habit of standing strong in your position and being clear and honest in your needs.

For the relationships that you are already in, focus on undoing your habits around staying quiet or not speaking up for yourself and start focusing on being actually heard by the other half in your relationships. This will take some time as you may have already developed unhealthy habits in your relationships, but the more you set the intention of working through them, the sooner you will be able to grow away from these habits.

Your Partner Needs to Be Emotionally Intelligent

As an empath, especially if you are entering a relationship with someone who is not an empath, you should be looking for emotional intelligence in people. People who are emotionally intelligent will generally have a better sense of control over their emotions, which means that they will be less likely to become harmful through their emotions. Rather than blowing up when they are angry, guilt tripping you when they are sad, or being overbearing with their jealousy, they will know how to manage their emotions and refrain from spilling them all over others. As an empath, this means that you can feel more confident around them and their ability to manage their emotions, thus meaning that you are less likely to become harmed through their poor emotional management.

As you enter new relationships, look to see how they handle their emotions in general. Avoid getting blinded by how they are treating you during the earliest stages of your relationship when they are likely trying to make a good impression and look for other clues instead. See what they say about how they have treated others in the past or experiences they have had with other people, and pay attention to how they treat those around you. If you see them spending time around their friends or family, pay close attention to their behavior because these are the relationships where they will act the most authentic to who they really are. If they are not kind, compassionate, or empathetic towards others in their life, chances are they will not be kind, compassionate, or empathetic towards you when you get closer to them. As a result, you can conclude that it may be a poor relationship for you to enter.

If you are in a relationship with someone who is not emotionally intelligent and who tends to spill their emotions everywhere, you are going to need to start asserting verbal and energetic boundaries. With your boundaries, you can start preventing their energy from leaking into your energy field and teach them to stop spilling all of their emotions onto you. While opening up and confiding in you is one thing, taking their emotions out on you or confiding in you if you have expressed that you do not currently have the time or energy to invest in listening is not okay. Assert this boundary and ensure that they respect it, or consider ending your relationship with this person if they don't.

Your Partner Needs to Be Considerate Of Your Needs

Lastly, the second half of your relationship, whether it is with a lover or a coworker, should always be considerate of your needs. If you plan on spending a lot of time around a person and investing energy into building a relationship with them, you need to make sure that they not only respect you but also consider you and your needs. A great example of someone considering your needs would be if you were to confide in someone about your sensitivities and then they asked you how you were feeling during high energy outings that you shared. This proves that not only will they respect your need to manage your energy, but that they will also consider your needs and ask about your feelings. Not everyone is going to show this level of consideration, especially if it is just an acquaintance, but if someone wants to be closer with you, they should express consideration for you and your needs in one way or another.

As you enter new relationships, look for people who show compassion and consideration for your needs as an empath. If they do, chances are that they are a kind of person who is going to think about you and be respectful of you as an empath. If they don't, they may be too self-absorbed for you to comfortably engage with given your unique needs. However, make sure that you are looking out for consideration and not service: you want someone who is considerate towards you, not a servant.

In your current relationships, look for the people who show true consideration towards you and nurture those relationships. In relationships with anyone who may not outwardly express consideration for you and your needs, consider whether or not they respect you and if you feel safe and cared for in your relationship. If you do not, or if you feel like you are consistently ignoring your needs for them, you might want to reconsider your relationship with this person.

Your Quick Start Action Step: Audit Your Relationships

Your quick action step today is to audit your relationships and start paying attention to where you can improve the relationships that you already have in your life. If you need to, start speaking up more and asserting your boundaries in your relationships more so that your loved ones can begin respecting you and your needs. If you have tried this and they continue to ignore you or refuse to change the way they treat you, you might consider ending your relationship with that person. It can be challenging to end relationships, particularly if you have a great deal of compassion and love for the other person, but in some cases, it is completely necessary.

Chapter 5: Coping Strategies for Empaths

Chapter 5: Coping Strategies for Empaths

Coping as an empath is probably one of the single most important things that you will ever learn about. With the right coping methods, you can ensure that you are not being overwhelmed by your gifts and having them run amuck on you. This way, you can always feel confident in your ability to stay in control over yourself and your energies even in the most challenging of environments. In this chapter, you are going to explore what your unique coping needs are, how to create your coping goals and strategies that you can use to begin coping better.

Your Unique Coping Needs

The first thing that you need to know is what your unique coping needs are as an empath. While the general purpose of coping will always remain the same, each empath may find that their unique needs are different based on how they experience their empathic gifts. In order to discover what you need in order to help you cope, you should start by considering the areas in life that you struggle with the most. This way, you can start to identify where coping methods may be needed based on what specifically is making your empathic gift so challenging to manage.

A great way to discover where your struggles are to refer back to your journal and start considering what is causing the most problems for you. Then, see if you can identify why and what part of your empathic gifts are being overwhelmed during those particular moments. You may find that you struggle most with dealing with other people's emotions or energies, or that you find yourself being dragged down by the collective energy of an environment in general. You may find that there are even specific people or types of people who are hard for you to be around but due to circumstances beyond your control, you may have to be around these people on a consistent basis. By identifying exactly where your empathic gifts become the most challenging, you can discover exactly what you need to do in order to overcome those challenges and experience greater success in managing your empathic gifts.

The Goal of Coping Strategies

Once you have identified where you struggle the most in your life, you need to start identifying what specific goals you want to be working towards so that you know what you are trying to achieve through your coping strategies. Your goals should directly align with your challenges outlined in the previous section to ensure that you are working on things that actually matter to your unique needs. If you have many areas of your life where you need to improve your coping strategies, consider starting with the parts of your life that pose the biggest challenges for you. That way, the relief that you are working towards has a massive impact on your life from the start, and you can move on to managing the less challenging but still difficult parts of your life after.

Coping Strategies for You to Try

There are many coping methods that you can try when it comes to coping with your empathic struggles. Some we have already covered in previous chapters, whereas, others will be discovered below. The more coping strategies you equip yourself with, the easier it will be for you to overcome challenges and move forward. Take your time and practice each of these coping methods, starting with the ones that serve your needs first and then moving on to learning how to incorporate the rest of these coping methods later.

Quiet Time Outside

As an empath, being in nature is a great way to cope with your daily challenges as nature tends to have a very healing and relaxing energy that is not present in crowded areas within society. As a general rule of thumb, retreating to be in nature at least once or twice a week is a great opportunity for you to completely ground your energies and restore your inner sense of peace. While you are there, you can either walk or simply allow yourself to be present in nature, or you can set aside some time to meditate and allow yourself to intentionally ground and bring in peace through your meditation. If you are someone who prefers comfort and familiarity, consider finding an area near your home that you can go on a regular basis, such as a forest or a riverside. Going to the same space each time can amplify its healing effect by helping you stay more focused and intentional while you are there. It can also help by having you know exactly what energy to expect while you are in the area so that the energy associated with "new" or different surroundings do not interrupt your grounding abilities.

Alone Time

As you know, solitude is one of the greatest tools that you can use when it comes to managing your energies and thriving as an empath. This coping method can be used by spending more time alone doing calm activities by yourself, or it can be used on-the-go if you are in need of a quick refresh from a challenging day. A great opportunity to tap into alone time on the go is by going outside for a few minutes, going to the bathroom for a few minutes, or even retreating to your office and closing the door for a few minutes when you need to. Giving yourself these few minutes of alone time will greatly help you relax and recharge after a particularly challenging time. Plus, you only need a couple of minutes to generate a sense of inner peace and restore yourself so that you can go about your day as usual and not feel so overwhelmed.

When you first start using short bursts of alone time to help you get through your day, you may feel like a few minutes is not enough and you are still overwhelmed when you go back to your daily routine. Trust that this is normal: you have not yet taught your mind and body to recognize that these breaks are a part of your new normal and that you will have another one soon. The more you use these breaks, the more your mind will be able to relax because it will trust that another break can be had soon if you feel that you need it again. This sense of inner trust cultivates a deeper sense of inner peace and will help you cope better overall.

Emotional Expression

As an empath, you pick up a lot of emotions from your day-to-day experiences, which is probably one of the most challenging parts of being an empath. Despite the fact that these emotions are not always yours, they are experienced as if they were which means that you need to practice proper emotional expression to help yourself release the emotions you carry. Some empaths like to express their emotions immediately, whereas, others like to use intentional expression time as an opportunity to express their emotions. However you choose to do it, make sure that you set aside time for you to completely feel and release your emotions.

The more you intentionally release your emotions, the less you will carry within you. This continuous expression prevents emotions and energies from building up within you so that your inner bottle does not remain "full," thus making further emotional experiences even harder to navigate. Instead, your inner emotional reservoir remains balanced so that you can experience new emotions without having them piggyback on others and increase your challenges in navigating your emotions.

Maintain a Healthy Lifestyle

One way to balance your empathic gifts is to maintain a healthier lifestyle and focus on your overall well-being. When we do not manage our general health, stress hormones like cortisol and adrenaline increase which can result in you feeling an intense amount of general overwhelm within. As a result, managing your emotions also becomes more challenging because you are experiencing so much overall stress.

As an empath, one of the biggest things you can do aside from eating a healthy diet, getting a good sleep, and exercising on a regular basis is to drink plenty of water. From a spiritual aspect, water is the element that resembles emotions and drinking water will help you move unwanted energy through your body and release challenging emotions from your system. Staying hydrated will not only help your general health, but it will also help with the passing energy and emotion through your system so that you can heal from your inner emotional challenges as an empath.

Try Yoga

Yoga is a profound and powerful way of navigating your energies and emotions as an empath. Yoga itself involves gentle exercise with meditation and intentional breathing to help move energy through your body and keep you in a calm and centered state of being. If you want to get everything you can gain from yoga, choose a particular style of yoga such as Hatha or Bikram yoga and commit yourself not only to engaging in the exercises but also in the learning of it. Each style of yoga features theory and education around energy, including the management and processing of energy, which means that a good yoga practice will help you stay in shape while also managing your empathic energies. This makes this an especially powerful form of activity for empaths to engage in.

If you are not overly confident in practicing yoga with a group of people, you may wish to incorporate yoga into your solitude practices. Spending time alone deeply engaged in a yoga practice can give you the restorative benefits of being alone alongside the benefits of yoga itself, which ultimately supercharges these two coping methods.

Use Guided Meditations

Guided meditations are another great way for you to manage specific types of energy. If you find yourself being bogged down by a specific energy, such as the energy of anger or envy, consider using guided meditations as an opportunity to help yourself release these energies and move on from them. YouTube is filled with plenty of great guided meditations that you can follow that range from fifteen minutes to sixty minutes in length. To engage in one, simply relax into a comfortable sitting or lying down position and turn one on then follow the instructions of the person guiding the meditation. It may take a few tries to find someone who has a voice that you can actually relax to, but once you do, you may find that this is one of your best coping methods yet.

The best part about guided meditations is that they tend to be extremely versatile and they can help you move through just about anything that you may be facing. If you feel that you do not currently have an effective coping method towards a specific type of energy, engaging in a guided meditation is a great opportunity for you to expand your skillset. As you do, you may find yourself naturally engaging in inner meditations any time you experience a specific type of unwanted energy, based on what you learned in a guided video. These guided meditations often feature visualizations that coincide with the releasing of unwanted energies, which is what makes them so powerful in the long run. The more you engage in them, the more visualization you will discover and the more likely you will be to discover a certain visualization that really helps you cope with certain energies. This way, you can simply recall that visualization practice and use it at any given time to help you through an energetic release, even if you are on the go.

Your Quick Start Action Step: Your Signature Coping Method

Now that you have a general sense of what you can do to cope with unwanted energies, it is time for you to develop your "signature coping method!" As an empath, one of the greatest things that you can do for your energy is to use a consistent routine when it comes to releasing unwanted energies. The reason for this is that, not only is it a good way to rely on things that actually work, but it also increases their functionality because your brain becomes used to associating particular coping strategies with an energetic release. As a result, your strategies will actually work quicker and will have a deeper impact on helping you release overall.

To develop your signature coping method, consider your goals once again and pick a strategy listed above that works best in helping you achieve that specific goal. Then, go ahead and begin practicing that method on a regular basis. As you do, you may find that you want to customize it to fit your needs a little better, which will help you make it *your* signature strategy. The more you practice it and personalize it for your own needs, the greater fulfillment you will gain from it, so make sure that you practice it on a regular basis. Notice how much more powerful it becomes as you do, and lean into that power to further enhance your ability to cope using your signature coping strategy.

Chapter 6: Protecting Yourself against Unwanted Emotions

Chapter 6: Protecting Yourself against Unwanted Emotions

As an empath, you need to learn how to properly protect yourself against unwanted emotions. Hopefully, you have already been practicing shielding and grounding yourself based on what you learned previously, so you already have a general idea of how you can protect yourself. However, you may feel as though these methods are simply not enough as your energy may continue to feel exposed or vulnerable in certain situations. For that reason, you will need to address your protective abilities and find new ways to protect yourself against unwanted energetic experiences.

In this chapter, we are going to explore how you can protect yourself by creating your own shielding and grounding strategies to really help you experience protection against unwanted emotions and energies. This way, you can feel empowered to take full control over your energy and experiences as you proceed through life. In this chapter, you will learn about a few different shielding and grounding techniques and you will discover when each style should be used. Then, you will be supported in creating your own signature shielding and grounding practice that you will call on any time you need a strong anchor to protect you against your environment or those around you. You should also keep this book handy so that you can rely on other strategies taught here just in case you find that your signature protective strategy is not quite enough in certain situations.

Different Types of Shields

Empaths have access to quite a few different types of shields that they can rely on should they need to shield themselves in public or high energy places. In general, there are three shields you will likely want to rely on in addition to the white energy ball shield that you have already been practicing until now. These include a mirror shield, a spike shield, and a brick shield.

A mirror shield essentially requires you to first create your white ball energy shield around you and then mentally line the outside of your shield with mirrors that are pointing outward. This shield helps send energy back where it came from, which ensures that if anyone is trying to throw negative energy your way, it is sent right back to them through your mirror. This way, people such as narcissists who may be trying to harm you are unable to because their energy is being redirected back towards themselves.

A spike shield is one where you create your white energy ball shield around you and then imagine it drawing big spikes in towards you and big spikes out towards the universe. This blur the edges of your shield and helps you "mix" with the energy around you better without actually allowing it to penetrate directly into your personal energy field. This is a great shield to use when you are trying to blend in better, such as in busy public environments.

A brick shield is made the same way, starting with a white energy ball and then ending in you visualizing the entire exterior of your shield being covered in bricks. Imagine as though you are building a brick box around yourself, keeping you safe inside of it. These shields can be quite extreme so you should refrain from using them unless you are going to be in an energetically dangerous environment, such as one that involves a narcissist. That way, absolutely none of their energy penetrates into your space and you can remain protected and away from their destructive energetic field.

Methods for Grounding Yourself

Like with shielding, there are also many ways that you can ground yourself and keep yourself protected from the energies that may accidentally penetrate into your personal space. Sometimes, shields can have energy leaks or the pressure of trying to keep others' energy out can result in you having intense energy building up inside of your own energy field. This can become exhausting and can prevent you from experiencing a clear and comfortable energy field, thus weighing you down and increasing the burdensome feeling of being an empath.

When it comes to grounding, there are three practices that you can do in addition to visualizing roots extending from your tailbone or your feet and penetrating the earth below you. One involves the earth, and two involve water which, as you know, is fundamental in helping you navigate emotions effectively.

The one involving the earth is also known as "earthing" and requires you to walk around outside barefoot for a few minutes. Ideally, you should be doing so on the grass or in the dirt as these are believed to be the purest form of earth energy, connecting you deeply to the ground below. As you walk, the idea is that the earth draws unwanted energies out of your body through the soles of your feet and supports you in maintaining a clean energy field.

Another practice you can try is using Epsom salt baths to cleanse your energy in. Water itself is known for being cleansing, and salt is believed to ward off negative energies that may be lingering in your energy field and leaving you feeling weighted down and exhausted. By having an Epsom salt bath for at least 30 minutes, you can draw out unwanted negative emotions and leave yourself feeling light and refreshed.

If you do not prefer baths, you may prefer this third practice: cleansing showers. Cleansing showers can be used in combination with a visualization practice to help you cleanse yourself of unwanted negative energies. To do so, simply step into a warm shower and visualize the water washing away any negative energies or emotions that appear to be trapped in your energy field. If you would like, you can close your eyes and visualize the water rushing off of you as if it were turning black from negativity, and you can continue visualizing it until it turns clear. The visualization of the water turning clear is indicative that all of the negativity has been washed away and that you are now cleansed and grounded from unwanted energies and emotions.

Creating Your Unique Protection

Formula

As with all forms of coping with being an empath and protecting yourself from external energies, you are going to want to generate your own unique protection formula to help you stay free of unwanted emotions. The best way to create your own formula is to start practicing the aforementioned shields and grounding techniques and to see what fits with you the best.

Below are the three steps that will help you in creating your own unique protection formula so that you can feel completely protected and grounded at all times.

Step 1: Practice All Methods

Practicing all of the protection shields and grounding practices outlined in this book is going to give you the best opportunity to try each shield on for size and get a feel for how it actually supports you in action. Each person will be drawn to unique strategies and will find that different practices work better for them or will fit better into their lifestyle, so do not be afraid to mix it up and see what fits best with you. You may wish to log your experiences in your empath journal so that you can recall how each shield and grounding strategy helped you and which one made you feel the best afterward. You should try using each method at least three times so that you can get a full feel for what the experience will be like. Otherwise, you may find yourself not benefiting as much simply because it can take some time to properly put the method to work and grow from it.

Step 2: Assess Your Unique Circumstances

Once you have practiced with creating your own shields and grounding strategies, you want to make sure that you are creating a signature protection method that is going to fit *most* of your life experiences. So, if you find yourself consistently being drawn into busy places and feeling vulnerable and exposed, you may benefit most from a spike shield. If you are regularly exposed to narcissists or energy parasites, you may benefit most from a mirror shield with the occasional brick inlay. If you live nowhere near nature, you may benefit more from grounding showers or baths instead. Find practices that are going to fit your unique lifestyle and needs and start using them on a more consistent basis so that you are building on practices that actually serve you. Remember, the more you practice a technique, the quicker and more effective it will be because your brain and energy become familiar with this consistent practice. As a result, the minute you start, you will begin to experience relief from it because it is being used so frequently in your life. This is why having a "signature" style is so important: because consistency truly is the key to developing protection against unwanted energies and emotions.

Step 3: Personalize Based on Your Intuition

As you go along, you may feel intuitively called to customize your protective and grounding methods so that you can experience full freedom from unwanted energy or emotions. Perhaps, you are inspired to include a mirror on your spikes, or you want to both shower and use a soap bar with Himalayan pink salt in it. You may even find yourself being called to meditate and ground next to live plants or do something specific when you are protecting yourself that your intuition calls you towards. Lean into this calling and exercise it, as your intuition will best guide you in the direction that you need to go when it comes to protecting yourself. Always trust your intuition.

Your Quick Start Action Step: Protect and Ground

Your quick start action step today is to begin practicing just one of the shields listed in this chapter. In doing so, you are going to start developing a feel for what each shield feels like and how it serves you best. Focus on using the one that is most likely to help you the most based on your life circumstances and commit to using it at least three times over the next day or two when you feel that you need to. This way, you can start practicing creating that unique shield and putting it to work. If you find yourself being intuitively called to add a new step, personalize it in some way or another, or do something differently, do not be afraid to lean into that intuitive calling. This will only help you create an even stronger shield, so it is well worth your time and effort.

Chapter 7: Empaths in the Workplace

Chapter 7: Empaths in the Workplace

Being an empath in a place of work can pose unique challenges that you may not have to face in other areas of your life. For most people, going to work is non-negotiable because you need to make money to survive and pay for your costs of living. If you have a family, that demand goes up even further as you have additional people that you have to care for. Even if you run your own company or you are self-employed, you are still going to have to deal with people out of obligation as a way to ensure that you are getting paid and earning an income. Due to the necessity of working so that you can make a living, work may add an additional stress into your life because you are not able to leave or recover from emotional or energetic overwhelm when you need to.

Understanding Your Unique Experiences

As an empath in the workplace, you are going to

experience unique challenges that those around you will likely not face themselves, which can make working in a standard work environment stressful. The average work environment is already a fairly stressful place, with many people being pooled together in one area and being forced to work together regardless of whether or not they actually get along. What can happen is that people have friction between them, work doesn't get done in time and people get blamed, or the overall environment becomes stressed out from having too many different personalities in one area. It is somewhat like a high school: everyone is there because they have to be, not necessarily because they want to be, and it can lead to many issues for everyone present.

As an empath, being in an environment where there is stress, blame, a lack of interest in being there, anger or aggression, and other emotions that typically arise in workers, it can be overwhelming. You may find yourself getting stressed or anxious just because of the general energy of your environment, even if you have no reason to be stressed out yourself. You may also find yourself resenting your workplace and feeling a deep dread towards attending work on a daily basis because of how stressful the environment may be. The fact that you resent it so much but you are obligated to go in order to earn a paycheck can also add to the overwhelm and stress, making it even harder for you to navigate the energy and emotion of your workplace.

Navigating Your Environment

Just because your workplace is hard to navigate does not mean it is impossible, remember that. With the right tools in place, you can easily begin navigating your workplace without feeling the deep sense of overwhelm and anxiety that may have taken over you in the past. It simply requires you to predict what the environment is going to be like and begin adjusting your energy and emotions accordingly so that you are no longer being hijacked by the energies of those around you.

The best way for you to begin navigating your workplace is to start by getting a general sense of what the workplace feels like on a regular basis. This overall energy that typically lingers in your workplace should be fairly consistent, even if the daily energies fluctuate from time to time. The easiest way to gauge this energy is to ask yourself what one to three describing factors come to mind every time you think about your workplace. You might think something along the lines of "cheerful, friendly, and overwhelming" or you might think more along the lines of "dark, dreadful, and angry." Each unique workplace will have its own energy so pay attention to yours and get as close to an accurate feel on the environment as you can.

Once you have gotten a general idea of what your work environment feels like, start considering the factors that lead up to the unwanted emotions and how you are impacted by them on a daily basis. Maybe it is a stressful boss, demanding customers, lazy coworkers, an overworked schedule, or a lack of reasonable pay that makes your job so stressful for you.

Highlight all of the reasons why you dislike your place of work so that you know exactly where your unwanted energies and emotions are coming from. Then, start to consider what ways you can manage these unwanted energies and emotions. For example, if it is because your boss is stressful or your customers can be rude, consider shielding yourself against their energies before you even get to work and keeping your shield carefully intact all day. Whenever they come in your presence, consciously reinforce your shield and affirm to yourself that you are not welcoming any unwanted energies or emotions into your space.

For things you can control, consider actively doing something about making a change for yourself so that you do not have to endure the challenges any further. Remember, even if it is uncomfortable, you still have the right to speak up for yourself and make a change in your own life. Do not be afraid to do things like ask for a raise or a promotion, seek a new job, assert your boundaries so that you no longer have to take on more work than normal, or tell your boss who was really at fault when work didn't get done. When you speak up for yourself, you reinforce the fact that you are not willing to be taken advantage of and that your energy and emotions must be respected. As a result, you are better able to take control of your workplace experience and minimize or eliminate the unnecessary stress that you experience as a result of your work environment.

Steps for Dealing with Others

There are a few things that you can actively try to help you assert your energetic and emotional boundaries in the workplace and stop being so overwhelmed by your workplace duties. Below are a few examples of what you can try to make your work life more bearable.

Step 1: Set and Assert Your Boundaries

The first thing that you can do to help you navigate your workplace more effectively is set and assert your boundaries so that people no longer have the capacity to take advantage of you. As an empath, setting boundaries can be challenging because you may fear what will happen if you set them. If you have been surrounded by narcissists and energetic parasites all your life, you may find this even more challenging because they have conditioned you to eliminate your boundaries.

The best way to set and assert your boundaries is to consider where your personal space is being intruded upon and choose to set a boundary there. For example, say you constantly have to do the work of two people because your coworker refuses to do their own work and you do not want to have to confront them or your boss on the lack of work being accomplished. Instead of being taken advantage of, you could declare that you are no longer doing work that is not rightfully yours and that your coworker needs to step up and complete their own tasks. If they don't, stand firm in your boundaries and do not be afraid to tell your boss about the real reason behind why work is no longer being completed. It may feel uncomfortable and you may worry that you will get in trouble, but if you calmly and respectfully assert your boundaries then you can ensure that you are not being taken advantage of by your coworkers or boss.

Step 2: Reinforce Your Energetic Shields

Whenever coworkers, customers, or workplace authorities enter your space who have low or bad energy, make sure that you consciously reinforce your energy shield. If you need to, imagine the white energy ball sweeping through your energy field starting at your core and moving out to your shield walls again as a way to "sweep" unwanted energy out of your field. Do not be afraid to put a mirror on the outside of it to help you deflect their energy and prevent it from coming into your personal energy field. That way, you can avoid carrying unwanted energy with you throughout the day.

Step 3: Take Advantage of Your Breaks

When you get your work breaks, make sure you use at least a portion of your break to relax completely and ground yourself from the energy of your day. If you can, leave your workplace for a few minutes just to get a break away from the overwhelming energies and use this as your time to relax from the overwhelm. Even just a few minutes outside breathing in fresh air and consciously grounding your energies can really help you release unwanted energies and stay refreshed throughout the day. If you need an impromptu break, consider excusing yourself to go to the bathroom and spend a minute or two running your hands under cold water and envisioning it washing away unwanted energies.

Your Quick Start Action Step: Coping in Your Workplace

Your action step today is to consider one area in your workplace that is particularly challenging for you and start consciously reducing the amount of stress that you experience through one of the coping methods mentioned above. Start simple by taking grounding energy breaks and reinforcing your energetic shields around yourself so that you can begin to feel safer in your work environment. Then, as you go, if you find areas of your environment where you need improvements, begin consciously and intentionally making changes so that you no longer have to face the challenges. If you cannot make immediate changes, start consciously setting yourself up so that you can make them in the near future. Sometimes, just having the hope that things are going to be different is plenty to help you relax and stop experiencing such intense overwhelm in your work life.

Chapter 8: Dealing with Emotional Parasites (Narcissists and Energy Vampires) and Toxic People

Chapter 8: Dealing with Emotional Parasites (Narcissists and Energy Vampires) and Toxic People

As an empath, you are particularly vulnerable to the challenges associated with being affiliated with people who are considered to be energetic parasites, such as narcissists and energy vampires. A combination of your sensitivities and your struggle to assert your boundaries can leave you especially vulnerable to these individuals, which can be dangerous for your energetic and emotional health. It is important that you learn to identify why you are vulnerable and how, and what you can do to minimize your vulnerability and protect yourself against energetic parasites.

Why Empaths Are Especially Vulnerable

Empaths are especially vulnerable around energetic parasites because they tend to be recognized for having the one thing that energetic parasites typically lack or crave: empathy. As an empath, you have an excess of empathy compared to other people which, to people like narcissists or energy vampires, means that you have plenty to take advantage of or share. Of course, neither of these parties will ever actually ask you if you are willing to share your energy or your empathy, they simply know how to manipulate you into giving it to them. Then, they take advantage of you and you are left facing the consequences of their vile actions and behaviors.

In addition to your empathy, energetic parasites know that you struggle to say no and that, if manipulated, you will also protect them and their need for your energy. Because of this, they play on your energy and your emotions in all of the right ways to ensure that you are not able to protect yourself and step away from their energetic and emotional abuse. As a result, you are left stuck in their vices, struggling to free yourself from their grasp.

Recognizing Narcissists and Energy Vampires

As an empath, you need to start being able to recognize narcissists and energy vampires in advance so that you can protect yourself against their dangerous behaviors and manipulative practices. There are many ways that you can begin identifying narcissists and energetic vampires, but it starts by realizing that they are two different challenges and they present themselves in totally different ways.

Narcissists are self-absorbed to the extreme, often taking advantage of anyone and anything that they can to make themselves appear better than they truly are. They will take advantage of empaths because they know that an empath will see into their inner damages and will have compassion for them, even though they have no desire to change. An empath may be attracted to narcissists because of their own inner desire to see the best in people or to heal people who experience damage deep within them. Unfortunately, the narcissist cannot be saved or healed so the empath finds themselves trapped in a web of abuse and often discovers that they are unable to save themselves.

You can typically identify a narcissist through:

- Constant self-references and a desire to make the conversation all about themselves

- Excessive fantasies of success and an apparent desire to do anything to make those fantasies their reality

- Constant compulsive lying about anything to make themselves appear better than they really are

- Name-dropping or other forms of bragging that helps them feel as though they are better than everyone else

- Exploiting their loved ones by embarrassing them or ridiculing them in public to make themselves appear better

- Smearing your name to those around you by stating that you are a liar or too sensitive so that no one believes you anymore

Energy vampires, on the other hand, are completely different from narcissists. Unlike the narcissist, who wants to exploit you for their own need to look good in front of others, energy vampires want to exploit you for their own need to feel wanted and appreciated. An energy vampire will constantly demand your time, make it feel like you have to pay attention to them, and treat you badly if you try to take the time to take care of yourself. A person can be both a narcissist and an energy vampire, or they can be just one or the other. Oftentimes, narcissists will be energy vampires, but energy vampires will not always be narcissists.

You can spot an energetic vampire through behaviors such as:

- Constantly requesting you to

spend time with them and getting angry with you if you decline

- Expecting you to overlook your own needs and desires in order to fulfill theirs

- Calling on you to assist them or be with them at unreasonable hours, without any valid reason (such as a real emergency)

- Never respects your boundaries; may overstay their welcome, intrude on your private life, or start snooping in your belongings

- Tells you every single detail of their life and expects constant attention and compassion, even if you are too tired to offer it

Dealing with Energetic Parasites

Dealing with narcissists and energy vampires can be particularly challenging because, oftentimes, you have deep feelings of the energetic parasite that keep you attached to them even if it is against your best interest. This is not necessarily a problem, as long as you are willing to realize that an energetic parasite should never hold a meaningful space in your life where they have the capacity to declare plenty of your time. For example, you can be friends with a narcissist or an energy vampire but you should not become best friends with one or pursue one as a romantic partner. Keeping energetic parasites at a distance can ensure that they are not able to take advantage of you or exploit your empathic gifts for their own selfish gain.

Some steps that you can take to respectfully but assertively establish space between yourself and an energetic parasite are listed below.

Step 1: Set Boundaries

The first thing you need to do when dealing with energetic parasites is to set boundaries. Energetic parasites are known for having difficulty respecting boundaries, whether they are narcissists or energy vampires, which is why it is up to you to create and assert these boundaries in order to protect yourself. Anytime you notice a boundary is being breached, be very firm in asserting your boundary and do not be afraid to dish consequences to those who are unwilling to respect your boundaries. Due to their nature, energetic parasites will attempt to protest your boundaries and push you back into your previous behaviors to avoid being cut off from your energy supply. You will need to stay consistent in asserting your boundaries anyways. If you need extra help, you can always rely on a non-energetic parasite friend to empower you to stay firm in your position and protect yourself. If you are worried about your safety, do not be afraid to bring in reinforcements or assert your boundaries in a very public place to avoid being harmed by the upset energetic parasite. If you need to, keep protection around you until they leave you alone so that you are not vulnerable to their abuse.

Step 2: Lower the Expectations

In your relationships with energetic parasites, always seek to lower the expectations that both of you have around the relationship itself. Do not expect energetic parasites to be able to change so that they can fulfill your fantasy of who you wish they were as this will only leave you feeling disappointed and stressed out when they never change. As well, reduce their expectations on what they can gain from your relationship so that they no longer see you as an easy target for them to fulfill their needs. The mutually reduced expectations can prevent either of you from relying on the relationship to provide more than what can reasonably be fulfilled by the other person. Getting the expectations lowered, especially on a mature relationship where you have been taken advantage of for some time, may be challenging at first. Make sure that you continue to assert your boundaries and lower the expectations until both of you are able to adhere to those lowered expectations and maintain them.

Step 3: Wean Off of Close Relationships with Them

If you are in a romantic relationship with an energetic parasite, your only way to fully end the energetic and emotional abuse is to completely leave the relationship. Unfortunately, these relationships will never change and you will continue to be exploited and harmed so long as you stay in the relationship. You may delude yourself into believing that you can manage, that you can adjust your approach to make the relationship better, or that it will somehow improve, but this will never happen. Instead, you will always be chasing something that can never actually happen because you are expecting too much from someone who simply does not have the capacity to offer you what you want or need.

If you are in a friendship or you are family with the person in question, consider weaning both of you off of the relationship until it is at a safe and comfortable distance. Only you can decide what that really feels like, so make sure that you take your time and simply continue lowering the expectations and asserting your boundaries until you find a comfortable balance. You will know that you have found it when maintaining your relationship becomes an act of self-care and an act of self-love rather than something that you do out of a sense of obligation to the other person.

Your Quick Start Action Step: Approaching Relationships

Your quick action step with approaching your relationships is to begin identifying any relationship in your life where you feel that you may be exposed to an energetic parasite. It may feel harsh or cruel to label them as such, but the reality is that people who are taking advantage of you both energetically and emotionally are just that: energetic parasites. Get clear on who these people are in your life and start enforcing the steps above to begin protecting yourself against them and their abuse.

The sooner you start cleaning up the existing relationships in your life, the easier it will be for you to refrain from getting into any future relationships with energetic parasites, too. Consider this the act of you intentionally and consciously raising your standards on how you are willing to be treated and then taking the necessary steps in order to raise those standards. The more you reinforce these new standards, the easier it will be for you to maintain them in all of your existing and new relationships. As a result, you will find yourself being exposed to fewer and fewer relationships with narcissists and energetic vampires because you are able to identify them and protect yourself immediately.

Chapter 9: The Benefits of Recharging Through Solitude

Chapter 9: The Benefits of Recharging Through Solitude

Empaths require solitude as an opportunity to recharge and protect themselves against the destructive energies of the world around them. In addition to being protective, solitude gives empaths the opportunity to connect with their own personal energy and get a deeper and more intimate feel for who they truly are. In this chapter, you are going to learn about the value of solitude and how you can start creating more solitude in your own life so that you can start feeling a greater sense of personal freedom and power in your life.

Why Empaths Require Solitude

Empaths require solitude because it enables them to both ground and protect themselves against external energies and generate a deeper relationship with themselves and their own energies. Regular access to solitude gives an empath the ability to know themselves on an intimate level, which makes it easier for them to tell their own energy apart from the energy of others in busier places. Because your personal energy is constantly evolving, regular access to quiet time ensures that you always stay clear on what your personal energy is. It also allows you to contemplate your personal energy on certain things that you may be facing in your life, allowing you to get a better sense for how *you* personally feel about the circumstances that you are facing.

In solitude, you can ground yourself from unwanted energies and emotions and start genuinely giving yourself the time and attention that you deserve. There, you can identify areas of your life where you can improve or better protect yourself, things that need to change, or relationships that may need to be adjusted so that you are no longer being exploited. In this solitude, you know that everything you are thinking and feeling is entirely your own and is not being manipulated or influenced by the energy of others. As a result, you can trust that everything you think and feel during this time is exclusively your own thoughts and feelings which ensures that you can rely on them as being truly your own.

What Counts as Solitude

Creating solitude in your life may feel challenging if you are consistently surrounded by people. If you are a part of a large family, for example, being alone in your home may seem virtually impossible. It may also seem like busy parks or populated areas are too overwhelming for you to truly be alone in. So, you may need to work a little harder in order to generate solitude in your own life.

For an empath, the solitude of being alone in a bedroom can be enough to give you the space that you require in order to protect yourself and engage in the healing and recharging benefits of solitude practices. For every day solitude, you may try things like:

- Taking a bath or shower with the

bathroom door closed

- Going to your bedroom, shutting the door, and declaring that you are to be left alone (you might play soft music to hush the sounds from outside of the door)

- Going for a solo walk through your neighborhood or at a local park

The aforementioned activities are a great way to generate solitude on a daily basis when complete solitude may feel too challenging for you to acquire. Still, you may find yourself craving complete solitude from time to time so that you can recharge and feel a deeper sense of calm and connection to yourself personally. For these more intentional forms of complete solitude, you might consider doing things like:

- Going for a solo hike (with the appropriate safety equipment)

- Attending a spa with private options like float tanks or Himalayan salt rooms

- Renting a hotel or an Airbnb and staying there by yourself for a night or two

Steps for Creating More Solitude

Creating more solitude as an empath is not always about having the resources to generate solitude but also the inner permission to actually engage in solitude. If you struggle to implement solitude practices in your life and find yourself constantly being surrounded and overwhelmed, try the following steps.

Step 1: Give Yourself Permission

The first thing that you need to do when it comes to generating solitude in your life is to actually give yourself permission to do so. Many empaths find themselves struggling to create alone time because they have devoted themselves to meeting the needs of everyone else and they struggle to fully commit to fulfilling their own needs. If you are a people-pleaser or feel like others deserve your time more than you do, you are going to need to start giving yourself the permission you need to fulfill your own needs to. Simply saying "I give myself permission to fulfill my own needs" and then acting on that permission is a great way to get started.

Step 2: Start Small

If fulfilling your own needs is challenging because solitude is hard for you, you may be an empath who is dealing with the issue of codependency. It is not uncommon for empaths who have been under the thumb of a narcissist or an energy vampire to struggle to give themselves permission to be alone and then actually go engage in alone time. For that reason, you might consider starting with something smaller that will be easier for you to engage in on your own. You do not have to do something drastic right off the bat, particularly if you struggle feeling comfortable by yourself. Spending an extra few minutes alone in the shower, going to your room to sit quietly by yourself, or going for a short walk around the block are all great places to start. You can do something more extravagant later on when you are feeling more confident in spending your time alone.

Step 3: Do Something That Actually Interests You

Just because something has been mentioned as a good way of spending time alone does not mean that you are required to actually do that. If you are not a fan of hiking, for example, do not feel as though you have to go on a hike in order to feel a sense of emotional and energetic freedom. Instead, focus on doing things that you actually enjoy and avoid doing things simply because someone else told you that you should. If there is something you can think of that was not listed, do not be afraid to do that and enjoy the benefits of being on your own as you engage in that activity. The more you do what you enjoy, the easier it will be for you to see the benefits of your solitude and start defending it more fiercely.

Your Quick Start Action Step: Incorporating Solitude into Your Routine

Today, your quick action step is to start improving your solitude routine so that you can gain the benefits of recovering and recharging during your own personal downtime. I want you to take just a few minutes today to spend on your own, either by sitting alone in your room for a while or going for a walk by yourself. If you have something else you would prefer to do in your own time, do that instead.

Then, before you bring your alone time to a close, you also need to schedule in a more secluded session for solitude. For example, book a hotel room or schedule a day off where you are going to go to a park or do something by yourself without anyone else around. This way, you start experiencing the immediate benefits of solitude through a daily practice and you begin experiencing the long-term benefits as well through your more elaborate solitude practice.

Chapter 10: Raising Empathic Kids

Chapter 10: Raising Empathic Kids

Empaths who become parents often go on to have empathic kids themselves, as well. The reason behind this is not exactly understood, so it is unclear as to whether empathic gifts are inherited, learned, or developed over time. Regardless of how this phenomenon spreads, it is still important that you understand that empathic children will have special needs compared to non-empathic children. Learning how to fulfill these special needs and serve your child in a whole-hearted way is important in helping them develop the skills required to cope with being an empath so that they can grow up as empowered empaths.

Recognizing Empathic Children

Identifying whether or not your child is an empath ultimately comes down to observing their behavior and getting an idea of how they behave in comparison to other children around their own age. Empathic children tend to be more sensitive than other children, and they may be more likely to experience things such as overstimulation or anxiety. An empathic child will also be more likely to be attracted to animals and the outdoors as they intuitively seek to connect with living beings and areas that bring peace to their energy fields. In addition to this gentle nature, your empathic child may also have a tendency to show a heightened sense of compassion for those around them, even if it seems as though the other person does not deserve it. Empathic children are often described as being emotionally mature in that they will continue to show compassion and concern for people, even if those people have repeatedly been mean towards them. It is as though they just know on some inner level that the other person is hurting and they desire to show that person compassion and care since they can sense that the other person is lacking that in their lives.

Empathic Children's Unique Needs

Empathic children tend to have all of the same needs as empathic adults, except that their needs may be more pronounced because they are younger and may not understand what is happening to them. They need to be shown how to manage the experience of sensing so many energies around them and protecting themselves against those energies. An empathic child will also need to be shown how they can develop and maintain boundaries and what that looks like. You will need to empower your empathic child to feel safe in asserting themselves and letting those around them understand their needs and ensuring that those needs are met. Of course, sometimes, they will be surrounded by people who do not understand them or their needs so you will need to guide them through the process of navigating these experiences too. As a parent to an empathic child, your job is a little more intense because you need to navigate all of the standard difficulties of parenting as well as the need to protect your child who is more sensitive than those around them.

Supporting Your Empathic Child

As a parent to an empathic child, you need to ensure that you are supporting your child in understanding themselves and cultivating the tools that they need in order to thrive as an empath. The same tools that you are learning to create protection within yourself are what your child will need to create protection around themselves, too. Of course, you will need to adjust how you teach these skills to ensure that you are teaching your child how to create protection around themselves in a way that they understand.

Step 1: Creating a Safe Sanctuary

The first thing you need to do when you know that you are raising an empathic child is to create a sanctuary for them to retreat to when they are feeling overwhelmed. There should be two sanctuaries that your child has access to you, and a safe space they can go to when they need to be alone and recharge in solitude. For yourself, you should seek to be compassionate, considerate, and empowering with your child so that they know that you will understand their needs and support them in difficult times. Keep your communication open and clear and do not be afraid to explain what they may be going through to them and how you can help them navigate it more effectively.

For their bedroom, consider making a quiet space that can be turned into a small sanctuary for them to retreat to if need be. Using soft lighting, a comfortable chair, and some quiet activities that they can calm themselves with, you can ensure that your child feels safe in their own space. Make it clear that this space is not only designed to be comfortable but that the energy in this space is comfortable, too. Allow them to be an advocate for their quiet space so that they can protect the energy of their space according to their own needs. In other words, if your child does not want certain people in their room, asks for quiet alone time, or needs a break for any reason, make sure they know that they will not be bothered in their room. Keep your voice quiet and calm in their room and show respect for your child's sanctuary at all times so that they know they can feel calm and confident there at any time.

Step 2: Equipping Them with Proper Protective Tools

In addition to creating a safe space within their room and with yourself, you should also seek to educate your child on how they can properly protect themselves so that they can become their own safe space, too. Some great tools that you can offer for your child include relaxing breathing, cleansing baths, and meditation practices.

Relaxed breathing is a great way to help your child relax on the go, particularly if they are feeling overwhelmed in any situation. Asking them to breathe in and push their belly out with their breath and then breathe out all of the way is a great way to teach them to center themselves. This way, your child can begin connecting back in with themselves and calming down any time they feel that their energy is getting overwhelmed.

For cleansing baths, give your child an Epsom salt bath (using the proper dilution ratio for their age) and help them by asking them to visualize the water cleansing away their unwanted energies. If they are particularly young, you can simply visualize yourself cleansing away their unwanted energies as they bathe to help them relax. This is a great way to start showing your child how to cleanse themselves energetically.

For meditation, you can adjust the way that you teach it based on how old your child is. However, a great practice that seems to work well for most ages is to ask them to breathe deeply and then start describing a visualization to them that helps them ground and shield themselves. The simplest way is to use the same white energetic ball shield that you use and ask them to imagine it sweeping all of the unwanted energy out of their energy field. This way, your child can ground and protect themselves at the same time.

Step 3: Asserting and Protecting Their Boundaries

Children are particularly vulnerable to not knowing how they can protect themselves against unwanted energies and emotions coming in from the outside world. The best way to ensure that they are protecting their boundaries is to explain what boundaries are to them and explain the importance of boundaries. Be sure to let your child know that even when it doesn't feel comfortable, asserting their boundaries is an important skill that they need to rely on in order to keep their energies and emotions safe. If ever your child feels that their boundary is being breached or that someone is not respecting their boundaries, make sure that your child knows to communicate this with you. This way, you are able to help them keep their energies safe when they are struggling to do it themselves, and your child never feels overwhelmed or alone with their empathic gifts.

Your Quick Start Action Step:

Helping Your Empathic Child

If your child is an empath, the first thing you need to do is schedule some time for you to watch them and consider their actions and behaviors and how they may be impacted by their gifts. Then, your next course of action should be to start creating safe spaces for your child. Begin by ensuring that their room becomes a safe space and that you become a safe space for your child as well. A simple conversation can be a great start for this, and then you can set aside some time to turn their room into a more relaxing space if they feel that they require this added relaxation.

Once your child starts recognizing you and their bedroom as being their safe spaces, you can start teaching them how they can become their own safe space as well. Show your child how to meditate and ground themselves, as well as educating them on how they can protect themselves against unwanted energies with shields and boundaries. In doing so, you teach your child that they not only have some great safe spaces to retreat to for help, but they also have some excellent resources to help them become their own safe space, too. This way, you are helping your child successfully manage their gift both in the immediate future and in the long run.

Bonus Chapter: Dealing with the Media

Bonus Chapter: Dealing with the Media

Empaths and the media are not always a great combination, especially when the media is filled with negative and traumatic stories that can lead to overwhelm in the empath's energy field. Everything from gossip to reports on tragedies can be challenging for an empath to deal with, making the media, in general, a tough thing for empaths to navigate. In this bonus chapter, you are going to discover how you can continue to coexist with the media in a more harmonious way to avoid feeling the burdens of the media itself.

Why the Media Is So Challenging

As an empath, you may feel like it is your duty to stay informed on worldly events so that you can, in one way or another contribute to the healing of the world around you. Even if you are not consciously aware of this fact, chances are this is the exact reason why you are struggling with watching the media, yet continuously feeling called to do so. Still, every time you watch it, you may be left feeling nauseous, anxious, depressed, devastated, or even traumatized from what you have seen. This is because even though the energy being cast is far away or even from a different timeline than you are currently in, the witnessing or reporting of the events that you are hearing about is enough to impact you. Your empathic gifts are triggered and, just like that, the media becomes just as troublesome as public places or high energy environments. In some cases, it may be even more troublesome because you do not just experience energy overload, but energy overload that stems from negative or traumatic energies. For that reason, the media is a challenging point of contact for empaths who are trying to navigate the world around them but either cannot or do not want to avoid it altogether.

Which Types of Media Will Impact You

As an empath, virtually every type of media will

impact you in one way or another, as all forms of media are energetically charged. Whether you are scrolling your timeline on social media and consuming content that your friends have written or you are watching the news on TV, any form of media will be overwhelming for you. In general, any media that is negative, filled with gossip, tragic, or traumatic will be overwhelming for you which will make it virtually impossible for you to pay attention without feeling overwhelmed.

Modifying Your Media Approach

In order for you to have a successful experience with the media without feeling incredibly overwhelmed or traumatized from your experience, you are going to need to modify your approach to consuming various forms of media. The best way to ensure that you are able to stay informed and connected without traumatizing yourself or feeling completely drained is to filter the way that you engage with the media around you. Below are three ways that you can start consuming media in a healthier way so that you can start feeling more empowered and informed, and less overwhelmed and depressed around the media.

Step 1: Change How You Consume Media

If you are someone who feels the need to stay informed but struggles to consume media without feeling overwhelmed or drained, consider changing the way that you consume media altogether. Instead of watching the news live or watching it in video format, consider choosing your preferred news website and going to that website to read the news whenever you want updates. This is going to help you stay more in control over your experience by ensuring that you are in control over when and how you are consuming content. This way, you do not have to watch the media at specific times, but instead, you can energetically prepare yourself and then consume the media at your own discretion, and at your own pace. As well, you can choose to read the news articles that are relevant to you or to what you want to know so that you can avoid consuming things that are too overwhelming or depressing. This way, you can still read the headlines of important information, but you do not have to graphically experience the information in a way that makes the traumatic energy even more challenging to navigate.

If you need to keep up to date on current events in the celebrity world, consider following reporters that are more uplifting and less focused on gossip and drama. Spending some time searching for people who are going to be able to serve the information to you in a way that is less aggressive or exploitative and more honest and to-the-point is worth the effort. In doing so, you can avoid the uncomfortable energy that comes from reading something that feels like a bullying text while still staying up to date with the latest goings on in the celebrity world.

Step 2: Clean Up Your Social Media

Your social media is another place where you can find yourself consuming unwanted media if you are not being careful, which can make social media a challenging experience. From people sharing tragic videos to people complaining about their lives non-stop, there is a lot of unwanted content that can be consumed on social media if you are not careful. As an empath, this content can be especially overwhelming and depressing, even more so with how quickly you are consuming it all as you scroll by. Even if you are not stopping to read the actual posts, the words themselves will stand out to you as you scroll and scan your feeds which will leave you feeling overwhelmed and depressed.

If you want to continue using social media without feeling so drained and overwhelmed after, consider being more intentional about who you follow and what posts you interact with. Stop following people who are consistently sharing graphic tragedies or complaints and focus on following people who are more empowering and uplifting. As well, make sure that you never interact with a post that features content that may leave you feeling depressed and unhappy because social media algorithms will see this interaction and show you more similar content. Instead, simply hit "hide post" or "unfollow" from that particular post and hide the content from your feed altogether.

The same goes for your email list: make sure that you take some time to unsubscribe from every newsletter that you get that you never open. Although they may not have any energy in terms of what they are saying to you, the constant blast of new newsletters into your inbox every day can be overwhelming and uncomfortable. Keeping your inbox clean of any unwanted newsletters (or unwanted energy) and only open to genuine conversations is important in helping you avoid overwhelm.

Step 3: Learn to Tune Out

You may find yourself using your phone as an opportunity to escape the external world around you, particularly if you are feeling overwhelmed by your physical environment. Unfortunately, most people will turn to social media in these times as a way to mindlessly scroll and keep themselves feeling distracted from the overwhelm. If you do this, you may realize that this does not actually keep you calmer, but instead, simply turns your attention to something less stressful. What it actually does, however, is increase the stress that you experience overall, because now not only are you experiencing environmental stress but you are also consuming stressful content on your phone.

If you want to experience greater relief, consider turning to coping mechanisms like deep breathing and meditation as a way to keep yourself feeling relaxed around overwhelming energies. This way, you are not increasing the amount of stressed out energies that you are actively experiencing in your life. Instead, you are decompressing and allowing yourself to fully cope and lean into your protective strategies, which actually makes them even more powerful because you are "exercising" them in your times of need.

Your Quick Start Action Step: Cleansing Your Media Diet

Your quick start action step around media is to cleanse your media diet! In your empath journal, write down every form of media that you are consuming that is leading to you feeling overwhelmed and exhausted. Then, get started on the process of changing the way that you consume your media so that you can still stay informed and in the loop but not at the expense of your own well-being. Turn off the news, find a reliable and honest news source, and start following their *website* (not their social media account) so that you can consume their content at your own pace. Anytime you begin reading their content, focus on reading it only when you are feeling energetically available to pay attention to everything going on in the media. The moment you feel overwhelmed, respect your own boundaries and disconnect so that you can feel complete relief before consuming any more. Do not read articles that are going to completely drain you unless absolutely necessary, but instead, simply see the headline and consider that enough. Consuming graphic or overly described content about tragedies or traumas can result in you overwhelming yourself and feeling unable to go about your normal daily experiences. If you truly want to help others around you, you need to be helping from an empowered space and not an overwhelmed space. From an overwhelmed space, you will be unable to help.

Next, pay attention to how often you are scrolling social media and exactly what you are consuming when you do. Unfollow pages and friends who are sharing content that makes you feel overwhelmed or drained, and delete or block anyone who continually attacks you personally on social media. That way, your social media experience is not needlessly draining.

Lastly, go through your email and make sure to unsubscribe from all of the newsletters that you do not enjoy receiving. If you need to, take a few days to go through the unsubscribing process so that you do not overwhelm yourself all at once. This way, your email inbox will remain clear and stress-free, too, which will ensure that your entire media experience is more relaxed and inviting.

Bonus Book Preview:

"Enneagram Self-Discovery: Easy-to-Follow Essential Guide on How to Uncover your Unique Path with the 9 Enneagram Personality Types to Build Self-Awareness and Achieve Personal Growth" by: Morgan Christopher Hudson

Chapter 3: The 9 Personality Types Explained

We are now beginning to get to the truly transformative portion of this book. You will now learn about the actual nine personality types that we have discussed, wing types, and of course, a Quick Start Action Step to get you on your way to growth and balance.

The main nine personality types are the Reformer, the Helper, the Achiever, the Individualist, the Investigator, the Loyalist, the Enthusiast, the Challenger, and the Peacemaker. But before we go into an overview of all nine types, their strengths and weaknesses, their fears, and their real-life examples, let's explore wing types. This is important to go over because your wing type can slightly alter your Enneagram personality type.

The reason for this is because every person is unique, we don't fit within a box. We can be a mixture of our dominant personality type, along with having traits from the personality type next to us. This means that if you are a Five, you could have traits of a Four or a Six. If you are a One, you might have traits of a Nine or a Two. The types that are next to our number are known as wings.

While your primary personality type will display the dominant traits, you may also have side traits from your wing type that add to your individuality. These side traits may complement your personality or appear contradictory. This is because people, and our personalities, are multi-faceted. We are not static or two-dimensional.

This means that you don't only need to consider your dominant type, but your wing type as well. Your personality as a whole, including your strengths, weaknesses, and fears will be best understood when you consider all of the applying factors. If you are a Six and find there are some areas of your personality that aren't explained, it may mean that those parts of you are due to your wing type of Seven or Eight.

While some people show only one wing, others may show only a few signs of having a wing type at all. Even rarer are people who are greatly influenced by not one, but both wing types.

Studies on people who have two prevalent wings have shown that this, while fully possible, is rare. In a sense, everyone has two wings, as there are always two personality numbers on your sides. But it is rare for someone to display traits of both of these wings. Instead, it is more common for one wing to lie dormant while the other one affects a person's personality.

This means that if you are a Three, you may have both One and Two next to your type, but only adopt aspects of one of these types. Whichever wing that your personality takes on can greatly alter how you function, your fears, and strengths. Eights with Seven wings are greatly different than Eights with Nine wings.

Many people, after studying the Enneagram, training, and growth have found that they developed a second wing. Meaning, that if they are a Six, they are displaying traits of both a Five and a Seven as well. This may be because after undergoing self-evaluation, psychological work, and spiritual growth, a person begins to mature and develops the ability to travel between the nine personality types including their other wing. Or it could be that as the person ages and grows that they specifically developed their second wing. Either way, this is a sign of growth and progress toward becoming more balanced and emotionally healthy.

Now that you understand what the wings are, let's explore the basics of the nine personality types of the Enneagram.

Type One: The Reformer

One is characterized by having a strong instinct for right and wrong. They are ethical, conscientious, advocates, and crusaders. Yet while they desire to make a change for the better, they are afraid that they might make a mistake along the way. Their high standards can lead to resentment, impatience, and perfectionism. But when emotionally healthy and balanced, a One is well-organized, noble, wise, kind, and discerning.

Main Fear: That they will be condemned, make mistakes, or be overcome with 'evil.'

One with a Nine-Wing Enneagram: The Idealist

One with a Two-Wing Enneagram: The Advocate

Real Life Examples of Ones: Celine Dion, Katherine Hepburn, Plato, Michelle Obama, Kate Middleton, Tina Fey, Meryl Streep, Jeanne d'Arc, Harrison Ford, Al Gore, Jimmy Carter, Martha Stewart, Hilary Clinton, Anita Roddick, Julie Andrews, Jane Fonda, Maggie Smith, Helen Hunt, Margaret Thatcher, Nelson

Mandela, Prince Charles, Emma Thompson.

Type Two: The Helper

The second personality type is known to be warmhearted, kind, empathetic, friendly, generous, sincere, sentimental, and self-sacrificing. However, they can sometimes be overly people pleasing, possibly giving false flattery and trying to gain acceptance. They can struggle to acknowledge their own needs and use the attention they gain from others to validate themselves. But when balanced, a Two can offer unconditional love and support. They are known to be incredibly selfless and giving.

Main Fear: They fear deep within their heart that they are unworthy of love and unwanted.

Two with a One-Wing Enneagram: The Servant

Two with a Three-Wing Enneagram: The Hostess/Host

Real Life Examples of Twos: John Denver, Pope John XXIII, Eleanor Roosevelt, Stevie

Wonder, Dolly Parton, Mary Kay Ash, Monica Lewinsky, Nancy Reagan, Martin Sheen, Arsenio Hall, Lionel Richie, Josh Groban, Ann Landers, Elizabeth Taylor.

Type Three: The Achiever

Threes are charming and self-assured, attracting a large crowd and are known as the life of a party. They are known to be energetic, conscious of status, competent, poised, driven, and diplomatic. Although an unhealthy Three is overly concerned with their image and what everyone thinks of them. They have a strong need to distinguish themselves and receive affirmation. This means that they can easily be overly competitive and obsess over work to an unhealthy degree. But when they are emotionally healthy, they can learn to accept themselves, become authentic, and are strong role models.

Main Fear: That they are 'nobody' with no personality, need, or significance. They often feel worthless and unneeded.

Three with a Two-Wing Enneagram: The Charmer

Three with a Four-Wing Enneagram: The Professional

Real Life Examples of Threes: Lance Armstrong, Lady Gaga, Elvis Presley, Bill Clinton, Prince William, Madonna, Whitney Houston, Tom Cruise, John Edwards, Muhammad Ali, Augustus Caesar, Anne Hathaway, Reese Witherspoon, Justin Bieber, Will Smith, Taylor Swift, Tiger Woods, Oprah Winfrey, Tony Robbins, Paul McCartney, Ryan Secrest.

Type Four: The Individualist

The Fourth personality type is known to be personable, honest, sensitive, reserved, self-aware, and creative. But they can also struggle with feelings of self-pity, moodiness, self-consciousness, melancholy, and self-indulgence. They may keep others at a distance to avoid feelings of vulnerability. A Four may even avoid society and feel distrust and disdain for it. Yet, when balanced, a Four is inspirational, creative, stable, brave, and strong. Fours enjoy being able to surround themselves with beauty, be freely creative, and focus on their individuality.

Main Fear: That they are 'nobody' with no personality, need, or significance.

Four with a Three-Wing Enneagram: The Aristocrat

Four with a Five-Wing Enneagram: The Bohemian

Real Life Examples of Fours: Hank Williams, Cher, Nicolas Cage, Tchaikovsky, Kat Von D., Angelina Jolie, Anne Frank, Billie Holiday, Bob Dylan, Prince, Amy Winehouse, Johnny Depp, Sarah McLachlan, Cat Stevens, Virginia Woolf, Jackie Kennedy, Tennesse Williams, Edgar Allen Poe, Leonard Cohen, Kate Winslet.

Type Five: The Investigator

Fives are known to excel when it comes to focus, concentration, and both processing and developing complex skills and ideas. They can be insightful, curious, innovative, independent, alert, and inventive. Although, these strengths can also lead to Fives becoming detached, intense, isolated, eccentric, high-strung, cynical of spirituality, and preoccupied with their mind rather than living in society. But, if a Five can learn to overcome their weaknesses, they can be pioneers of thought, imagination, science, and more. They have a unique ability to see the world in a new way, which often puts them ahead of their time.

Main Fear: Being incompetent, incapable, useless, and helpless.

Five with a Four-Wing Enneagram: The Iconoclast

Five with a Six-Wing Enneagram: The Problem Solver

Real Life Examples of Fives: Emily Dickinson, Mark Zuckerberg, Gautama Buddha, Bill Gates, Albert Einstein, Stephen

King, Alfred Hitchcock, Tim Burton, John Nash, Agatha Christie, Vincent van Gogh, Glenn Gould, David York, Stephen Hawking.

Type Six: The Loyalist

The sixth type is known for being committed, reliable, cooperative, responsible, trustworthy, and hard-working. They are wonderful at foreseeing potential problems and then troubleshooting in order to solve it before it occurs. Their downfall is that they can become highly stressed, anxious, defensive and evasive. All the while, they often complain about it to those around them. A Six can struggle with suspicious, self-doubt, indecisiveness, rebelliousness, and are defiant. But, when a Six is emotionally healthy, they can be incredibly self-reliant, stable, and encourage all those around them.

Main Fear: Losing guidance or support

Six with a Five-Wing Enneagram: The Defender

Six with a Seven-Wing Enneagram: The Buddy

Real Life Examples of Sixes: Julia Roberts, Ellen Page, Robert De Niro, Prince Harry, Malcolm X, Mark Twain, Princess Diana, Eminem, Marilyn Monroe, Tom Hanks, Chris Rock, Sigmund Freud, Meg Ryan, Jay Leno, Mel Gibson, Jennifer Aniston, Hugh Laurie.

Type Seven: The Enthusiast

Sevens are known to be full of optimism and spontaneity. They can be extroverted, spirited, and playful. Yet, they are also versatile and practical. These traits, when unbalanced, can lead Sevens to become distracted, scattered, over-extended, and undisciplined. They are constantly seeking out new acclivities and distractions, which leaves them exhausted and anxious. They are unable to sit still, leaving them impulsive and impatient. But, when a Seven is emotionally healthy and balanced, they are great achievers and talented. They can truly enjoy life and feel satisfied.

Main Fear: That they may be deprived or experience pain.

Seven with a Six-Wing Enneagram: The Entertainer

Seven with an Eight-Wing Enneagram: The Realist

Real Life Examples of Sevens: Amelia Earhart, Elton John, Katy Perry, Fred Astaire, Bruce Willis, Howard Stern, Robert Downey Jr., Thomas Jefferson, George Clooney, Simon Cowell, Leonardo DiCaprio, Brad Pitt, Joe Biden, Galileo Galilei, Cary Grant, Chuck Berry, Mozart.

Type Eight: The Challenger

Eights are known for being resourceful, decisive, assertive, self-confident, and straight-forward. Although, they can also be domineering and selfish. An Eight will feel that they must control their entire environment, including their work, personal life, and relationships. This can lead to them becoming intimidating, confrontational, and loose tempers. They do this in order to protect their own heart and emotions, but in the process, end up pushing everyone away. Buta balanced and emotionally healthy type Eight can learn to be inspiring, generous, self-controlled, and brave.

Main Fear: Being controlled or harmed.

Eight with a Seven-Wing Enneagram: The Maverick

Eight with a Nine-Wing Enneagram: The Bear

Real Life Examples of Eights: Franklin D. Roosevelt, Paul Newman, Alex Baldwin, Rosie O'Donnell, Winston Churchill, Donald Trump, John Wayne, Dr. Phil, Martin Luther King Jr., Serena Williams, Queen Latifah, Russell Crowe.

Type Nine: The Peacemaker

Nines are often characterized by their warm and friendly personality. They are supportive, optimistic, trusting, accepting, creative, and stable individuals. However, they can become easily complacent with situations, as they are overly willing to keep the peace. Even if that false sense of peace is detrimental. A Nine's deepest desire is to be free of conflict. They desire everything to go smoothly and will tend to minimize the effect of anything problematic that they wish to ignore. A Nine is often willing to stubbornly allow their life to become stagnant rather than choosing an uncomfortable or confrontational approach to fix things.

When a Nine is emotionally healthy and balanced, they can be wonderful true peacemakers. Even if a situation is difficult, they can be willing to face it in order to address the issues. They shine at bringing people together, embracing differences, and standing their ground.

Main Fear: Separation and Loss

Nine with a One-Wing Enneagram: The Dreamer

Nine with an Eight-Wing Enneagram:

The Referee

Real Life Examples of Nines: Zooey Deschanel, Queen Elizabeth II, Walt Disney, Abraham Lincoln, Claude Monet, Ronald Reagan, George W. Bush, Gloria Steinem, James Taylor, Jimmy Stewart, Toby McGuire, Morgan Freeman, Audrey Hepburn, Janet Jackson, George Lucus, Carl Jung, Whoopie Goldberg.

Your Quick Start Action Step

Now that you understand what wing types are and the basics of the Nine Enneagram personality types, you can better understand what your individual type is and how it affects you. You should already know what number your type is. Now, it is time to find and understand your wing types. Schedule time this week to study up on your wing types on both sides of your personality, and see how one, or both of them, might be influencing you.

Chapter 4: The Three Main Centers Explained

The nine Enneagram personalities are divided into three groups, each containing three of the personality types. These groups are known as Centers. There is the Instinctive Center which contains Eight, Nine, and One, the Feeling Center with Two, Three and Four and lastly, the Thinking Center with Five, Six, and Seven. Knowing which Center you belong in is as simple as knowing which personality type you are.

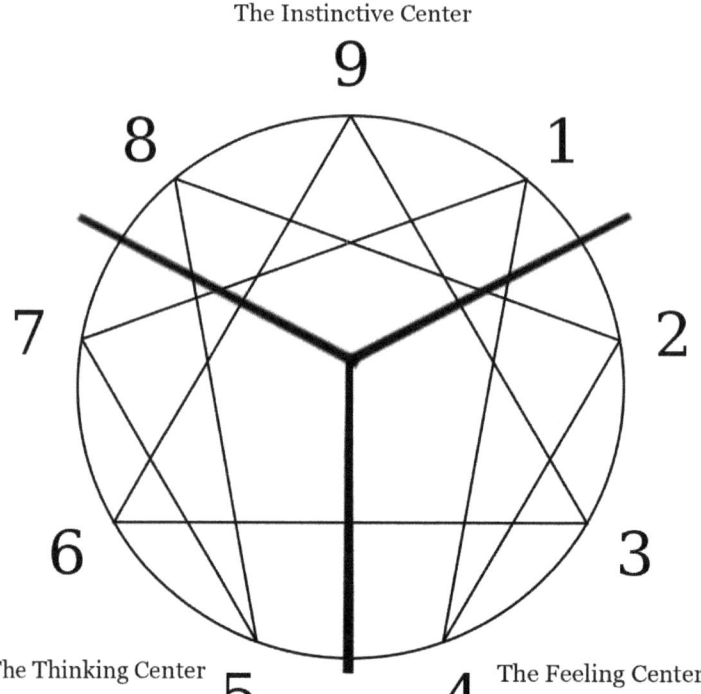

Each of these Centers and their personality types share specific traits. These traits may not always be obvious, but they are there. This is because each of the Centers and their personalities, known as Triads, has a collection of characteristics. These characteristics largely are subconscious, but can greatly affect a person. For instance, anger is common in the

Instinctive Center. Shame is mostly felt by the Feeling Center. Lastly, Fear controls the Thinking Center. All nine personality types may experience these feelings and emotions. But a given emotion will most affect a person who's in a Center connected with it.

In order to see how this is all connected, you need to learn about the heard, the heart, and the belly.

Riso and Hudson, those who developed the well-respected and most accurate form of the Enneagram test, have theorized about the Three Centers and Triads. Their theory is that each of the nine Enneagram personality types is a direct result of a specific imbalance within the three Centers.

We aren't born with this imbalance. Instead, we are born in a state of balance and emotional well-being. While in this state, we are in-tune with our true nature and able to access the Essence within all three Centers.

When we are in this natural state and our

Centers are balanced, then we are able to access all of the Essential qualities and live at a high level with ease. But then, we naturally develop an ego in order to survive within a difficult, harmful, and painful world. This development of the ego causes us to lose contact with part of our being, which causes much pain and damage to our psyche. Therefore, the ego attempts to compensate by developing its own way of staying into contact with the Essence.

The Centers are named for the Essence which the ego is responding with pain toward losing contact with. They can respond to this loss by manipulating energy within the Center in three different ways. This includes under-expressing energy, overexpressing, or both under and overexpressing in the case of personalities that have been the most disconnected.

The Belly/Instinctive Center

The Belly is all important, as it allows us to function in society. This Center of Intelligence is vital in order to interact with people, move and flow in life, and attain our goals. This Center controls our instincts and is what enables us to be truly connected to our bodies. Many cultures have explored the connection between our instincts, feelings, and our belly. In Qigong, it's believed to be our source of willpower, vitality, and confidence. In Buddhism, it is respected as our source of intuition, intention, and will. Even Western researchers are now calling the belly the "second brain." They have partly named it thus because its nervous system is nearly of the same complexity as the human brain. But they have also found that it is greatly responsible for emotional regulation with the production of endorphins and serotonin.

To learn more about this book and how it can help improve your personal growth, check out "Enneagram Self Discovery" by

Morgan Christopher Hudson.

Conclusion

Thank you again for owning *Empath Self-Discovery*!

I hope this book was able to help you to discover exactly what it means to be an empath and how you can live your life as an empowered empath. Being an empath in today's world is not always the easiest thing because there tends to be a lot of stress and overwhelm in our modern society. You might find yourself overwhelmed by the amount of exposure that you face by being constantly surrounded by people and things that are particularly overwhelming. From a stressful work environment to a negative social media feed, the demands of being an empath in a modern world can be particularly challenging.

Now, you should feel confident in using the tips you have discovered throughout this book to help you have a deeper sense of understanding around your personal energetic experiences and what they mean for you. If you are still struggling, trust that consistent application of your protective and grounding practices will help keep you safe and protected against unwanted energies. The more you practice these protective methods, the more powerful they will be in helping you release yourself from the grips of challenging demands placed upon you by society.

If you find that you have a particularly challenging area in your life, such as with energetic parasites or bullies in the workplace, make sure that you keep this book handy and refer back to it often. Keeping your knowledge and inspiration recent in your mind can ensure that you remain empowered to act against the troubles that you experience as an empath. This way, you are more likely to remember the importance of protecting your energies and asserting your boundaries, especially around people who have a tendency to ignore them and take advantage of you.

The next step after reading *Empath Self-Discovery* is to begin continually applying the skills that you learned within this book. It is not enough to simply know about them, but you need to consistently apply them, even if it seems like they are not working for you. In your lifetime, chances are you have spent a long time getting used to being an empath who has been taken advantage of and silenced in favor of other, louder individuals who steamrolled you. It is important that you realize that overcoming these challenges takes time as you need to both educate and empower yourself and educate and adjust the way others treat you. As you speak up and assert your protective shields, people may grow frustrated with you and try to bully you back into taking their abuse or sabotage so that they do not have to change their own behaviors. Realize that this is not a reflection of you not deserving to be treated better or that you are somehow failing yourself when it comes to creating and asserting your boundaries and protection. Instead, it is a sign that it is working because your own boundaries and shields are starting to be recognized by those around you. Stand firm in your position, stay consistent in your practices and trust that in due time, everyone will realize that you are serious about your needs.

Over time, you will grow stronger at asserting yourself and people will grow to recognize that you are serious about wanting to be treated better by them. As a result, the mutual understanding will lead to you being treated better overall and no longer having to lie down and let others treat you poorly. Instead, you will be able to live your life as an empowered empath because the balance of your life will come back in your favor. From there, you will remain in control over how you are treated forever and you will have the confidence and skills to prevent unwanted experiences going forward. As long as you continue to empower yourself and stay confident in your abilities, you will continue living your life being personally in control over your own energetic and emotional experiences.

Thank you and good luck!

www.ingramcontent.com/pod-product-compliance
Lightning Source LLC
Chambersburg PA
CBHW051547020426
42333CB00016B/2146